Morning Meditation

50 Days of Daily Inspiration

Ava-Gay Blair

MORNING MEDITATION. Copyright © 2019 by AVA-GAY BLAIR.

All Rights Reserved. No portion of this book may be reproduced, stored in a retrieval system, or transmitted in any way or form without the written permission of the author (mechanical, electronic, photocopying, recording or otherwise).

Scriptures taken from the Holy Bible, New International Version®, NIV®. Copyright © 1973, 1978, 1984, 2011 by Biblica, Inc.™ Used by permission of Zondervan. All rights reserved worldwide. www.zondervan.com. The "NIV" and "New International Version" are trademarks registered in the United States Patent and Trademark Office by Biblica, Inc.™

Scripture quotations marked NLT are taken from the Holy Bible, New Living Translation, copyright 1996, 2004, 2007. Used by permission of Tyndale House Publishers, Inc. Carol Stream, Illinois 60188. All rights reserved.

Scripture quotations marked KJV are from the Holy Bible, King James Version (Authorized Version). First published in 1611. Quoted from the KJV Classic Reference Bible, Copyright 1983, by The Zondervan Corporation.

ISBN: 978-1-949343-55-7 (paperback)

The Lord **GOD** hath given me the tongue of the learned, that I should know how to speak a word in season to him that is weary: he wakeneth morning by morning, he wakeneth mine ear to hear as the learned.

(Isaiah 50:4 - KJV)

I am not an ordained evangelist, teacher, minister or prophetess, but I do have a gift to encourage, enhanced by a word of knowledge.

Ava-Gay Blair

Acknowledgement

Finally!

This book is well over-due. Many have waited patiently to get a copy of this book in their hands. I am extremely grateful for all those who have encouraged me to put these "powerful words" I bring out daily on radio and Facebook in a book.

Glory be to God for downloading His words of inspiration into my spirit every morning to share with His people. I have yielded to the call for a time as this, with a mandate to uplift, encourage and help to pull persons out of hopelessness and shine my light for them to see and come to know Him.

Thanks to my family for their support and prayers over the years.

I am truly thankful to God for my boss, Wyatt K.C. Davis, who continues to see great potential in me and has been encouraging me along the way.

Special thanks to my Facebook viewers, radio family and all those who took the time out to share with me how my meditations have impacted their lives.

Introduction

I keep running out of papers and ink in my pens to write all these meditations daily. Now they are printed in a book, just for you. In this book, you will find 50 daily words of inspiration.

Each day you take up this book to read, prepare your mind to be receptive to the word for that specific day. Even though the book says "morning", you can choose to meditate on these words any time of the day. The meditations are written with the intention to engage the reader in a personal way. The words in this book are pointing directly to you, so you may find that the word "you" is used a lot for that personal experience.

This book intends to give you a boost of daily encouragement as you face life's challenges. It may speak loudly to your specific situation and cause you to relate and find hope in the messages. Many of the topics inside this book are similar to the ones you may have heard me share during my radio programmes or Facebook live sessions, but the contents give a fresh revelation.

There are specific songs that I have suggested for you to listen softly while reading the meditations. You can choose to listen the song before, during or after the meditation. Soon you will be able to own a copy of the Morning Meditation on CD. This is Volume #1 of many to come. Keep an eye out for more and more books of *Morning Meditation*.

If you are growing weary, read this book.

If you need a Rhema word, read this book.

If you just want your faith to be lifted, keep reading this book.

If you complete this book before the other volume is complete, then start again for another revelation and inspiration. The second time around will give you a fresh insight. Try it.

Get ready to be inspired!

Get ready to be encouraged!

Get ready for a daily shift!

Contents

Acknowledgement vii
Introduction ix
Day 1: God Is About to Break His Silence 15
Day 2: There's An Agitator In My Flesh 17
Day 3: When Victory Is In The Air, Defeat Draws Near 20
Day 4: Humble Yourself And Pray 23
Day 5: You Can Seek It And Lose Him
But If You Seek Him You Won't Lose It 27
Day 6: Running On Empty 30
Day 7: God Will Multiply What You Surrender 33
Day 8: Why Sit Here And Die? 36
Day 9: The Devil Has A Plot But Jesus Has A Plan 40
Day 10: He's the God Of Order 44
Day 11: You Are Bleeding 48
Day 12: The Devil Desires To Sift You 51
Day 13: Make Room For Your Breakthrough 55
Day 14: You've Won The Fight But Still In The War 58
Day 15: Someone Is Assigned To You 63
Day 16: If He Breaks Your Heart It Is To Save Your Soul .. 66
Day 17: Take Your Eyes Off the Enemy 69

Day 18: Press Some More 73
Day 19: Stay The Full Course 77
Day 20: Can God Trust You? 80
Day 21: Who Am I To You? 84
Day 22: It's Not A Mistake But A Design 88
Day 24: He Will Have To Cover You To Show You 92
Day 25: Internal Struggles Interfere With External Battles .. 96
Day 26: Provision Is In The Place Of Your Assignment 100
Day 27: No Valley, No Mountain 104
Day 28: You May Have To Lose To Win 107
Day 29: The Devil Is Always A Liar 110
Day 30: Your Transition Works With Time 113
Day 31: It Will Soon Make Sense 117
Day 32: Keep Gathering Sticks 122
Day 33: No Purpose, No Peace 126
Day 34: Persistence Breaks Resistance 130
Day 35: You Are In It To Come Out 134
Day 36: Who Authorized You To Surrender? 138
Day 37: The Devil Doesn't Want What You Have 142
Day 38: Love Them Still 146
Day 39: What You're Feeding Is Growing 150
Day 40: God Won't Bless That Mess 154
Day 41: Where You Sow You May Not Reap 158
Day 42: You Can Grow Among Thorns 163
Day 43: When God Gets Silent 166

Day 44: Stretchable But Not Breakable 169
Day 45: Show Him Where You Buried It 173
Day 46: Let Down Your Tail................................. 177
Day 47: The In-Time And On-Time Move 182
Day 48: Don't Surrender In A Fight You've Already Won 185
Day 49: What Do You Have In Your House?..... 189
Day 50: If You Don't Talk To God, Then Who? 192
Who is Ava-Gay Blair? 195

Day 1
God Is About to Break His Silence

(SONG TO LISTEN: SPEAK INTO MY LIFE BY MICAH STAMPLEY)

The LORD shall go forth as a mighty man, he shall stir up jealousy like a man of war: he shall cry, yea, roar; he shall prevail against his enemies. I have long time holden my peace; I have been still, and refrained myself: now will I cry like a travailing woman; I will destroy and devour at once. (Isaiah 42:13-14 - KJV).

God is about to judge it Himself. He is about to speak on your behalf. He is about to reveal Himself in all the confusion. The Almighty God is about to say something on the matter; that thing concerning you.

He has seen the works of the enemy against you. You have been enduring long enough. God is about to speak. The earth will tremble, things will fall back in line and the enemy will scatter. His words will fill that void. Confessions will come. Revelation is coming on that matter in secret for years. Too many have been silent and because God has not said anything yet, they think He agrees with their evil works. Your deliverance and breakthrough have been silenced but God is about to bring revelation through His word. When God speaks, there will be conviction. When God speaks, there will be assurance. When God speaks, there will be manifestations.

The men brought the woman who was caught in the act of adultery to Jesus. They wanted to hear what Jesus had to say on the matter, but Jesus stooped down and started writing on the ground with His finger as if He did not hear them. They really wanted to hear what He had to say, so they kept on pressing Him. He got up and spoke and it stirred up their emotions and convicted their hearts, "**He that is without sin among you, let him first cast a stone at her.**" (John 8:7 - KJV). After a while, everyone dropped their stones and started leaving one by one.

God is about to speak and send away your accusers. Don't lose hope, your word is coming. God will speak.

Day 2
There's An Agitator In My Flesh

(SONG TO LISTEN: GOD KEPT ME BY HEZEKIAH WALKER)

Who is an Agitator? An Agitator can be a person who urges others to protest or rebel.[1]

What does this Agitator want from you? Your Agitator wants you to give up.

An Agitator puts you in motion by shaking or stirring you up. An Agitator can stir up others against you. This Agitator seeks to disrupt your comfort and stretch your faith; that one person who will cause trouble or provoke you to wrath.

Do you know of one in your life?

The Apostle Paul called his Agitator **"a thorn in the flesh."**

> ...there was given to me a thorn in the flesh, the messenger of Satan to buffet me, lest I should be exalted above measure. For this thing I besought the Lord thrice, that it might depart from me. And he said unto me, My grace is sufficient for thee: for my

---
[1] Lexico.com

> *strength is made perfect in weakness. Most gladly therefore will I rather glory in my infirmities, that the power of Christ may rest upon me. Therefore, I take pleasure in infirmities, in reproaches, in necessities, in persecutions, in distresses for Christ's sake: for when I am weak, then am I strong. (2 Corinthians 12:7b-10 - KJV).*

How many times do you get this kind of response when you go to the Lord about your Agitator? That troublemaker is trying to drive you insane and instead of just taking it away, God says: *"My grace is sufficient for thee: for my strength is made perfect in weakness."* Paul said he pleaded with the Lord three times to take it away but He gives the same response. Can you relate? You too have prayed and fasted about it but it's still in your flesh and God is only helping you to endure.

Your Agitator is a part of your process. This Agitator is important on the journey to your destiny and what God wants to reveal to you. Many gifts are birthed through Agitators. Sometimes if there is no "thorn" in your flesh, you would never fall to your knees and pray. God gets much of your attention when something is in your flesh. So, the Agitator is not so bad after all and that is why God says His grace is sufficient to keep you. You must endure.

Hannah had Agitators in her flesh because of her barrenness. Her provokers pushed her to seek the face of the Lord for her breakthrough. Sometimes your Agitator will lead you to your spiritual gifts, because you spend more time seeking the face of the Lord about your trouble.

I know you are tired now and want it to just go away, but it will when it no longer becomes a fear, discomfort or distress. See it as your motivation to soar. Don't allow it to rob your joy while you endure. You shall not go crazy.

> *For God hath not given us the spirit of fear; but of power, and of love, and of a sound mind. (2 Timothy 1:7 - KJV).*

This Agitator may stay long enough just to make you stronger, but just remember, God's grace is sufficient to keep you.

Day 3
When Victory Is In The Air, Defeat Draws Near

(SONG TO LISTEN: I MUST BE CLOSE- MARVIN SAPP)

You must be close to what God has in store for you. Close to His plans that no eyes have seen nor ears have heard, because here comes more trouble. Stand strong, defeat draws near because you are nearer to something great.

The opposite of defeat is victory. The two do not agree or stay comfortably in the same mind. Defeat and victory are not friends. You cannot try to entertain both at the same time, no matter how you feel. Be careful of defeat, it will try to attach itself to your victory. At the brink of your breakthrough you will find the most oppositions. You won't experience complete victory if you keep allowing defeat in. You will have the victory in your hand, but still feel defeated.

When victory is near, setbacks, delays and disappointments will increase. This process can confuse your decisions and discourage you. There will be times when you don't feel victorious, but you must still believe you are. Defeat is a matter of the mind and not your reality. It is trying to hide your victory.

> *Put on the whole armor of God, that ye may be able to stand against the wiles of the devil. Above all, taking the shield of faith, wherewith ye shall be able to quench all the fiery darts of the wicked. And take the helmet of salvation, and the sword of the Spirit, which is the word of God. (Ephesians 6:11, 16 & 17 – KJV).*

You must be ready to stand against defeat at all times. The battlefield is in the mind, so you need the **helmet of salvation** and the **shield of faith.**

Never confuse your victory with defeat. Don't allow defeat to cause you to believe you will never win. So, as you are faced with another battle, another uncomfortable experience, you think it must be defeat, No! Most victories are birthed through trial.

> *My brethren, count it all joy when ye fall into divers temptations; knowing this, that the trying of your faith worketh patience. (James 1:2-3 – KJV).*

The Scripture did not say temptations will produce defeat. Keep on declaring your victory, walk victoriously, even in the face of defeat. If in that moment when you are rejoicing the enemy sends something to discourage you, declare victory. If in that moment when you are believing

God's report and the doctor's report starts to manifest, still declare victory.

> *Be sober, be vigilant; because your adversary the devil, as a roaring lion, walketh about, seeking whom he may devour. (1 Peter 5:8 – KJV).*

You won't see the victory if you expect defeat. When you walk in defeat you will never see beyond today; you will never see a brighter day; you will never see the good in the circumstance. You won't be victorious with a defeated mindset.

> *A double-minded man is unstable in all his ways. (James 1:8 – KJV).*

God gives complete victory. Don't allow defeat to rob your victory.

> *The thief cometh not, but for to steal, and to kill, and to destroy: I am come that they might have life, and that they might have it more abundantly. (John 10:10 - KJV).*

Abundant victory is yours today. Keep walking in victory no matter how close defeat comes.

Day 4
Humble Yourself And Pray

(SONG TO LISTEN: BRING ME DOWN BY THE GRACE THRILLERS)

> *If my people, which are called by my name, shall humble themselves, and pray, and seek my face, and turn from their wicked ways; then will I hear from heaven, and will forgive their sin, and will heal their land. (2 Chronicles 7:14 - KJV).*

If you humble yourself, pray, seek and turn, then heaven will respond; sins will be forgiven, and the land will be healed. There is a principle to the way we ought to pray to get heaven to respond. You can't go before God in pride, completeness and self-sufficiency. You must go before God empty, broken and ready to listen and move in obedience. Take off your authority and independence when you come. This should be your attitude when you come: *"God you are everything. You are high and mighty. The king of Kings and Lord of Lords. Your holiness consumes mine."* Humble yourself in prayer. Do not let pride hinder the flow of communication.

> *Humble yourselves in the sight of the Lord, and he shall lift you up. (James 4:10 - KJV).*

There is something about humility that gets God's attention.

> Two men went up into the temple to pray; the one a Pharisee, and the other a publican. The Pharisee stood and prayed thus with himself, God, I thank thee, that I am not as other men are, extortioners, unjust, adulterers, or even as this publican. I fast twice in the week; I give tithes of all that I possess. And the publican, standing afar off, would not lift up so much as his eyes unto heaven, but smote upon his breast, saying, God be merciful to me a sinner. I tell you, this man went down to his house justified rather than the other: for every one that exalteth himself shall be abased; and he that humbleth himself shall be exalted. (Luke 18:10-14 - KJV).

Don't wait on God to cause you to be humble. Learn to humble yourself.

> God resisteth the proud, but giveth grace unto the humble. (James 4:6b - KJV).

Come down when you are talking to God. Get low, so grace can be given. Take off your badges of honour, titles and achievements. God will not try to compete with you. Seek His face humbly and He will hear you from heaven and forgive and heal. The nation is in trouble because of prideful prayers. Breakthroughs are delayed because of prideful prayers. You can't hear from heaven without humility. If God sends you, don't question the kind of work He wants you to do and the kind of people He is sending you to. Don't allow pride to block or stop the move of God over your life. Are you one who challenges God with works you have done and the years you have been of service to Him, as if you could have been elsewhere doing other things? If so, it is time to humble yourself and pray.

David was so humble within himself that he was willing to acknowledge his sins.

> *Have mercy upon me, O God, according to thy lovingkindness: according unto the multitude of thy tender mercies blot out my transgressions. Wash me thoroughly from mine iniquity, and cleanse me from my sin. For I acknowledge my transgressions: and my sin is ever before me. Against thee, thee only, have I sinned, and done this evil in thy sight. (Psalm 51:1-4a - KJV).*

Many refuses to acknowledge their sins to a God who knows all things. So, the sin is hindering the move of God, but you are not humble enough to acknowledge it. Now you have been at the same place praying about the same thing for years without results. You have wronged someone, but you just can't find the boldness to say, "I am sorry." You want to fight back but God requires you to humble yourself and pray and He will do something you can't do.

Day 5
You Can Seek It And Lose Him But If You Seek Him You Won't Lose It

(SONG TO LISTEN: TOO MUCH TO GAIN BY SEBASTIAN BRAHAM)

You can lose God seeking it, but you won't lose it seeking Him.

> But seek ye first the kingdom of God, and his righteousness; and all these things shall be added unto you. (Matthew 6:33 - KJV).

He already knows your needs, so if you seek Him first, He will supply the things you seek. Everyone is seeking something to be satisfied. The Lord is seeking too:

> God is a Spirit: and they that worship him must worship him in spirit and in truth. (John 4:24 - KJV).

The devil is seeking too:

> Be sober, be vigilant; because your adversary the devil, as a roaring lion, walketh about, seeking whom he may devour. (1 Peter 5:8 - KJV).

You should be seeking too:

> *Ask, and it shall be given you; seek, and ye shall find; knock, and it shall be opened unto you. (Matthew 7:7 - KJV).*

If you want to secure what you seek, seek it in God.

> *But lay up for yourselves treasures in heaven, where neither moth nor rust doth corrupt, and where thieves do not break through nor steal. (Matthew 6:20 - KJV).*

If you seek Him first, you will find it all in Him. Anything you seek on your own, you will lose; but anything you seek through Him, you will find.

> *If any man will come after me, let him deny himself, and take up his cross daily, and follow me. For whosoever will save his life shall lose it: but whosoever will lose his life for my sake, the same shall save it. (Luke 9:23b-24 - KJV).*

God could be allowing you to lose some things to seek them again through Him. That way they will last. Therefore, this restoration you are seeking is to lose it in order to find it again in God. Job, after losing everything, worshipped.

> *Then Job arose, and rent his mantle, and shaved his head, and fell down upon the ground, and worshipped, And said, Naked came I out of my mother's womb, and*

> *naked shall I return thither: the* LORD *gave, and the* LORD *hath taken away; blessed be the name of the* LORD. *In all this Job sinned not.* (Job 1:20-22a - KJV).

Don't allow your losses to affect your worship. God still deserves it. Job's focus was on seeking God in his losses. If the way he came into this world was the way God wanted him to leave, then so be it. Job was willing to stand his losses seeking God. Are you willing to lose what you have to find what you should have? I don't know what you have lost, but maybe it is God's way of saying, "Seek me to find it back."

The rich young ruler asked, *"Good Master, what good thing shall I do, that I may have eternal life?" (Matthew 19:16b).*

> *Jesus said unto him, If thou wilt be perfect, go and sell that thou hast, and give to the poor, and thou shalt have treasure in heaven: and come and follow me. But when the young man heard that saying, he went away sorrowful: for he had great possessions. (Matthew 19: 21 - 22 - KJV).*

Not many are willing to lose to gain in Christ; to lose the world and gain salvation. But if you can't seek Him first, what is added will not last. Whatever you are seeking, seek God first to find it, because you can lose Him seeking it, but you won't lose it seeking Him.

Day 6
Running On Empty

(SONG TO LISTEN: FILL ME UP BY TASHA COBBS)

One of the most dangerous condition to be in, is to know you are on empty but operate as if you are filled up; being presumptuous on nothing. Pride has caused many to keep running on empty.

> *Blessed are they which do hunger and thirst after righteousness: for they shall be filled. (Matthew 5:6 - KJV).*

Experienced motorists know they should not risk running on empty, as that can damage their vehicles. What is the fuel needle saying in your soul? Is it on 'E'? If it is, how much farther do you think it will take you? Stop risking your life on an empty tank; you never know when you will break down or stop functioning. It costs much to keep gas in your tank, but it will cost you more if you keep running on empty. Your vehicle, just like you soul, will send out warning signs when you are on empty and need to be filled up.

Are you preaching, teaching, singing, filling others up but on empty? When a believer is on empty, he or she knows. Something doesn't feel, look or sound right. Most times you go through the motions and try to hide the emptiness. You still encourage those who come to you, but you too need a recharge. God knows when the vessel is dry and needs power.

Cornelius was a devoted man. He and his household feared the Lord. He gave to people and prayed always. In all this, the Lord knew Cornelius was running on empty. He was a prayerful man, but he needed to be filled up. The Lord sent Peter to him with the word and Cornelius, upon being filled up with the word, was also filled with the Holy Ghost. (See Acts 10: 1, 2, & 44).

It will cost you more if you take too long to be filled up. You want to serve the Lord but there are things in your way, so you choose to continue on empty. Romans 6:1 asks, *"Shall we continue in sin, that grace may abound?"* (KJV).

A Mechanic will tell you that a vehicle that continues to be used on empty will be in a bad condition. How much longer do you plan on chancing the journey on empty? Your spiritual fuel is running low, but you think you have to keep working, because no one else is there to do it. God would rather you stop to rest, than continue on empty.

> *These people honour me with their lips, but their hearts are far from me. (Matthew 15:8 - NIV).*

Do not ignore the warning signs. Your inside feels dry and things are not functioning as they used to. Don't chance another mile on empty; you may shut down. Even the enemy knows when you are empty and will take advantage of you in the process. This is what happened when some men showed up empty:

> *And the evil spirit answered and said, Jesus I know, and Paul I know; but who are you? And the man in whom the evil spirit was leaped on them, and overcame them, and prevailed against them, so that they fled out of that house naked and wounded. (Acts 19:15-16 - KJV).*

The woman of Samaria in her emptiness said, "Give me this water so that I will never be thirsty or have to keep coming here to draw water." (See John 4:15). She got excited about this infilling because Jesus said:

> *But whoever drinks the water I give them will never thirst. Indeed, the water I give them will become in them a spring of water welling up to eternal life. (John 4:14 - NIV).*

If you surrender your emptiness, then God will pour into you.

Day 7
God Will Multiply What You Surrender

(Song to listen: Lord I Surrender by Jermaine Gordon)

There was a certain widow who was in debts up to her neck. She was in distress, as her only son would be taken into slavery if she could not repay. This woman needed a miracle. What do you do when you have nothing to do? What do you do when you have nothing left? You surrender what you have to the Lord. Elisha asked her, "**What do you have in your house?**" (See 2 Kings 4:2). Oh yes, you are weeping but God wants to know if you have something to surrender for Him to multiply. A Preacher once said: "If it doesn't meet your need, then it becomes a seed."

Even when we have something, we call it nothing. The woman replied: "I have nothing in my house except a pot of oil" but that was just enough to surrender to the Lord. Without hesitation, Elisha sent her to borrow vessels from her neighbours, because God was about to multiply the little she surrendered. The song writer penned it this way: "Little is much when God is in it." Surrender the little you have, and watch God multiply it.

After she gathered all the pots and was told to shut the door behind her, the oil started flowing. There was no pot left to pour oil into. The one jar of oil supplied several jars with oil. It took one thing to multiply into many. She made a business out of the provision and paid off all her debts. The oil never ran out. When the increase comes from God it will last.

> *The blessing of the LORD, it makes rich, and he adds no sorrow with it. (Proverbs 10:22 - KJV).*

When you surrender what you have, it must be done by faith.

> *But without faith it is impossible to please him: for he that cometh to God must believe that he is, and that he is a rewarder of them that diligently seek him. (Hebrews 11:6 - KJV).*

A hungry multitude was before Jesus, but the disciples only found a little boy with five loaves and two fish. That was enough to surrender for the Lord to multiply. After Jesus blessed the meal, it multiplied; feeding five thousand men and leaving twelve baskets of crumbs. (See Matthew 14:13-21). God will make it stretch. He will cause it to be sufficient.

What do you have before you today that you want the Lord to multiply? You must first surrender it; without worry or doubt. Elijah said to the widow: "bake me a cake first." (See 1 Kings 17:13). Giving up your last is never easy but that sacrifice could be all it takes to receive all you need. It is a sacrifice because it cost you something. The woman was obedient and fixed the meal for the prophet first. She never ran out of flour nor oil after that.

There is always something in your house, hand or life to surrender. There is always something before you that you are calling nothing much but it is just enough to surrender. You won't see the value of what you have until you surrender it to the Lord. You won't see its ability to stretch until the Lord gets it. When you dedicate the insignificant to God, it becomes significant. It will stay longer than its expiration date when it is surrendered. If you surrender it, God will take it from there. The song writer said: "...Oh what needless pain we bear, all because we do not carry everything to God in prayer."

Day 8
Why Sit Here And Die?

(SONG TO LISTEN: IT'S NOT OVER NOW BY GLACIA ROBINSON)

It's not over. It's not finished. It's not ending.

> *Why art thou cast down, O my soul? And why art thou disquieted within me? Hope in God; for I shall yet praise him, who is the health of my countenance, and my God. (Psalm 43:5 - KJV).*

Do not bury yourself here!

There was a famine in the land and three leprous men began to reason within themselves and question their seemingly hopeless state: "Why sit we here until we die?" (See 2 Kings 7:3). They were faced with a choice to either stay there, go back into the city or go forward. Any decision they made could be life-threatening for them.

> *If we say, we will enter into the city, then the famine is in the city, and we shall die there: and if we sit still here, we die also. Now therefore come, and let us fall unto the host of the Syrians: if they save us alive,*

> *we shall live; and if they kill us, we shall but die. (2 Kings 7:4 - KJV).*

When you think you are falling into the hand of your enemies, you fall into the hand of God.

What condition are you sitting in right now that may be threatening your health: physically, mentally and spiritually? You are trying to decide if you should stay, go back or go forward, but all the options could threaten your life. Will you take a faith risk? Will you take a leap of faith and move into the unknown, in hope that God will lead you on or will you sit there and die? The choice is yours. You never know what God could do for you, if you sit there in hopelessness. You will never see the miraculous if you keep fearing the unknown. When will you get up?

> *And they rose up in the twilight, to go unto the camp of the Syrians: and when they were come to the uttermost part of the camp of Syria, behold, there was no man there. For the LORD had made the host of the Syrians to hear a noise of chariots, and a noise of horses, even the noise of a great host: and they said one to another, Lo, the king of Israel hath hired against us the kings of the Hittites, and the kings of the Egyptians, to come upon us. Wherefore they arose and fled in the twilight, and left their tents, and their horses, and their asses, even the camp as it was, and fled for their life. (2 Kings 7: 5-7 - KJV).*

These were only four leprous men who caused the enemy to flee. When you make a decision to get up in faith and go forward into the unknown, God will cause your enemies to flee from before you. Never doubt the power of your faith. God will move with you, when you move in Him. What the enemy left behind became the riches of the four leprous men. Did you know that "the wealth of the sinner is laid up for the just?" (See Proverbs 13:2) Why sit hopelessly in poverty, when wealth is ahead of you?

Why sit here until you die, when your faith can lead you into the provisions of God? You never know what lies ahead when you sit in hopelessness. Hope thou in the Lord! Who told you that you would die if you go forward? Sitting here has gotten you nowhere. Now, what lies ahead could be your victory.

> *What doth it profit, my brethren, though a man say he hath faith, and have not works? Can faith save him. But wilt thou know, O vain man, that faith without works is dead? (James 2:14 &20 - KJV).*

Examine your spiritual condition today. Are you physically dying or spiritually separated from God but continue to sit in sin? You must recognize your state and make a decision to either move forward and live or sit there and die.

The Prodigal Son knew he was not where he belonged.

> *And when he came to himself, he said, how many hired servants of my father have*

bread enough and to spare, and I perish with hunger! I will arise and go to my father, and will say unto him, Father, I have sinned against heaven, and before thee. (Luke 15:17-18 - KJV).

The Prodigal Son knew if he stayed where he was, he would not survive, so he got up and went back home in humility. You don't have to stay there and die. If and when you arise and move forward, you will see a way of life set before you.

Day 9
The Devil Has A Plot But Jesus Has A Plan

(Song to listen: Show Me Your Way by Heritage Singers)

When the devil plots, Jesus plans. What is the difference?

A plot can be described as something illegal or harmful that is devised and done in secret. On the other hand, a plan can be described as preparation or anything developed in advance to achieve something. (Lexicon.com)

So, while the devil makes harmful, secret plots, Jesus prepares to achieve something good from them.

> But as for you, ye thought evil against me; but God meant it unto good, to bring to pass, as it is this day, to save much people alive. (Genesis 50:20 - KJV).

Jesus' plans will always develop in advance, while the enemy's plots are, most times, devised on spot.

> Be sober, be vigilant; because your adversary the devil, as a roaring lion, walks about, seeking whom he may devour. (1 Peter 5:8 - KJV).

The devil cannot read your mind, so he may wait until you reveal something to him, to plot around it; but the omniscient God plans ahead of his devices. So, while he plots to overcome us, God has already made a plan of victory.

If you choose to serve the devil, you will always be plotting your way through life. If you allow him to use you, then you will find yourself scheming and devising plots to harm secretly, instead of planning to achieve something that can benefit yourself and others. Plotting will lead to lying, stealing and cheating.

> *He was a murderer from the beginning, and abode not in the truth, because there is no truth in him. When he speaketh a lie, he speaketh of his own: for he is a liar, and the father of it. (KJV John 8:44b - KJV).*

But God has a plan:

> *"For I know the plans I have for you," declares the LORD, "plans to prosper you and not to harm you, plans to give you hope and a future." (Jeremiah 29:11 - NIV).*

If you allow the Lord to use you, then you will find yourself planning rather than plotting through life. He will change the devil's plots to plan. He will work out His good will in all the works of the enemy against you.

> *And we know that all things work together for good to them that love God, to them*

> *who are the called according to his purpose. (Romans 8:28 - KJV).*

Study the wiles of the devil, so you can be aware when you are plotting or planning. You must know if you are devising evil works or your steps are being ordered by God.

> *In their hearts humans plan their course, but the LORD establishes their steps. (Proverbs 16:9 - NIV).*

> *Commit to the LORD whatever you do, and he will establish your plans. (Proverbs 16:3 - NIV).*

Plan with God and don't plot with the devil. The enemy plots to steal, kill and destroy, but God's plan declares life more abundantly *(See John 10:10)*. The enemy's plot causes weapons to form, but the plan of God won't cause them to prosper. While the devil seeks whom he may devour, God will cover you under His feathers and under His wings you will find refuge and His truth shall be your truth and buckler. *(See Psalms 91:4)*. While the enemy plots to sift Simon as wheat, Jesus prayed for him in His divine plan that his faith may not fail *(See Luke 22:31-32)*. So, for every plot there is a plan to counteract it. Glory be to God!

Look out for the counterfeit plot to the plan of God. It will look like the plan of God, but it is the plot of the enemy. Do not fall into the trap of plotting. If you find yourself creating havoc in the lives of others through lies, deception, and conspiracy, it is not of God. Be a planner, not a plotter.

Day 10
He's the God Of Order

(SONG TO LISTEN: ORDER MY STEPS BY BROOKLYN TABERNACLE CHOIR)

Just stay in line...You don't have to push or cut in. God will get to you. There is no way around Him. None can pay their way through Him.

> *For God is not a God of disorder but of peace. (1 Corinthians 14:33a - NIV).*

The KJV says:

> *For God is not the author of confusion, but of peace.*

There is a principle to be observed; things must be done in His order to work for you.

> *Ask, and it shall be given you; seek, and ye shall find; knock, and it shall be opened unto you: For every one that asketh receiveth; and he that seeketh findeth; and to him that knocketh it shall be opened. (Matthew 7:7-8 - KJV).*

He is a God of order, so:

> *...seek ye first the kingdom of God, and his righteousness; and all these things shall be added unto you. (Matthew 6:33 - KJV).*

God's order must be followed. You can't tweak it to fit your desires. Simon, the sorcerer, saw the Holy Ghost being given at the laying on of hands by the Apostles and he offered them money for the power they had, but Peter rebuked him (See Acts 8:18- 20). His heart was not right before God. When your heart is not right, you will struggle to follow God's order. If it is not God's way, it will lead to destruction.

> *Enter through the narrow gate. For wide is the gate and broad is the road that leads to destruction, and many enter through it. But small is the gate and narrow the road that leads to life, and only a few find it. (Matthew 7:13-14 - NIV).*

It is very easy to fall out of God's order when you start to seek things your own way.

> *There is a way which seemeth right unto a man, but the end thereof are the ways of death. (Proverbs 14:12 - KJV).*

When you miss the real instruction and the full revelation, you will miss the order. Many have quoted this verse over their lives from time to time for coverage:

> *No weapon that is formed against thee shall prosper; and every tongue that shall*

> rise against thee in judgment thou shalt condemn. (Isaiah 54:17a - KJV).

However, not many read the rest of it that says:

> This is the heritage of the servants of the LORD, and their righteousness is of me, saith the LORD. (Isaiah 54:17b).

There is an order to it. Here is another popular one:

> And we know that all things work together for good...

It continues with an order saying:

> ...to them that love God, to them who are the called according to his purpose. (Romans 8:28 – KJV)

Too many want the prosperity, coverage, provision, and protection, but living a reckless life before God. There is peace, joy, prosperity and safety in the order of God.

The Israelites were instructed to put the blood on their door posts to be saved from the death angel. I believe that some Egyptians followed the principle and were also spared from death. When you follow the principle, you follow the order and once that is applied, you will be safe. It doesn't matter who you are, I believe once the order is observed, you will receive from God.

I have heard it said that with God, when you are next in line, you are not waiting in an order that runs vertically that may have you waiting at the back, while others are ahead of you. However, this order could be horizontal, where you are lined up next to each other and anyone's name could be called out at any time. Stay in line. Stay in God's order. You don't have to become jealous, impatient or cheat your way through or be in a hurry to leave. The father had to remind the son who stayed of this:

> ...thou art ever with me, and all that I have is thine. (Luke 15:31b - KJV).

There is an order in place for the one who stays with the Lord; all God has belongs to you. What He has for you will come to you. God's order follows His perfect time and will. He is never late, and He never lies. He may interrupt your order to establish His in your life, because:

> A man's heart plans his way, but the LORD directs his steps. (Proverbs 16:9 - NKJV).

What you are waiting on will come to you in time. If you do not grow weary, you will reap. It is just God's order.

Day 11
You Are Bleeding

(SONG TO LISTEN: WOUNDED SOLDIER BY HELEN BAYLOR)

You are wounded and bleeding. Admit it! You are losing blood and it is not a case for doctors.

You are smiling, but bleeding.

You are preaching, but bleeding.

You are teaching, but bleeding.

You are singing (in ministry), but bleeding.

You have been wounded; it may be self-inflicted or caused by another. That wound needs some attention before it is infected, break out or even start to smell.

What are you struggling with that no one knows about and may never know about?

It is really uncomfortable when you are bleeding and everyone around you knows; so many keep silent in their conditions. As an influential person, you are assumed strong and unbreakable. If some people know you are bleeding, they may lose confidence in your ministry, expertise or advice. So, even in your condition you continue to work. You find no time to stop, rest and heal. You can't be bleeding and ministering to bleeding people; no one is being healed here. How can you fix others effectively, when you need fixing? You have a wound that needs attention; stop ignoring it. You need someone to administer healing to you too. Someone may find out about it and ask you to roll away the stone, because the condition is going for days and may have started to smell.

> *Jesus said, "Take away the stone." Martha, the sister of him who was dead, said to Him, "Lord, by this time there is a stench, for he has been dead four days." (John 11: 39 - NKJV).*

God already knows the state of your condition, just roll away the stone. What is stink to you is bearable for Him. He knows it has been there for some time now, but He will restore life to it.

You are losing too much blood; it is time to give your wound some attention. It is recommended that every counsellor, should have a counsellor. When you pour into others, you need someone to pour back into you.

How much longer do you think you can bleed and survive? After twelve years of bleeding, a certain woman could not take it anymore. She was weak, frail and, maybe, the talk of the town. She found herself in a public space, pressing her way to Jesus through a thick crowd for a healing touch. She was healed the moment she made contact with Him.

(See Luke 8:43-45). She risked her life just to put an end to her bleeding. The law said that a bleeding woman is unclean and who ever touches her is unclean and she should stay away from people. (See Leviticus 15:19-28). What are you willing to put aside to put an end to your bleeding? Your condition may be opened to them, but you could also be healed before them. Cry out for help, if you have to.

Blind Bartimaeus refused to let Jesus pass by without attending to his condition. Many will try to silence you in an effort to get you to accept your condition, but you have to be determined to reach for help. Blind Bartimaeus cried out even more: "thou son of David, have mercy for me." (See Mark 10:46- 48). If you continue to impart to others while bleeding, you may cause others to bleed. Take the time to attend to yourself first.

If you see a wounded soldier, administer healing. Many may seem well, but bleeding. They are not dead, just bleeding. The wounded can be healed. God will reveal what is beyond that smile. Too many wounded-bleeding soldiers are dying. Don't be the next or cause any one to die in their condition. Don't pass it on. I am sure you don't want another bleeding generation.

Bleeding families + Bleeding marriages = Bleeding children.

Take the time to dress your wound and start administering healing to another.

Day 12
The Devil Desires To Sift You

(SONG TO LISTEN: GREATER IS COMING BY JEKALYN CARR)

And the Lord said, Simon, Simon, behold, Satan hath desired to have you, that he may sift you as wheat: But I have prayed for thee, that thy faith fail not: and when thou art converted, strengthen thy brethren. (Luke 22:31-32 - KJV).

The devil is asking to sift you as wheat. He is coming to sift you as wheat. He may sift you as wheat; but Jesus prayed for you.

Many of you may have started experiencing the sifting, others may be coming out of a sifting experience, but it will happen to you at some point in your life.

God may allow fire to burn you, He may allow the earthquake to shake you and the devil to sift you, but in all this remember that Jesus prayed for you.

The enemy is requesting your life; he is requesting your peace and joy.

You are rejoicing too much in his sight; even when there is nothing to rejoice about. So, he is asking for a chance to sift you.

> *But put forth thine hand now, and touch all that he hath, and he will curse thee to thy face.* And *the* LORD *said unto Satan, Behold, all that he hath is in thy power; only upon himself put not forth thine hand.* (Job 1:11-12a - KJV).

This was a conversation between the Lord and the devil about Job. Job was sifted after this very conversation. The Lord allowed it because He trusted Job to endure to the end. Can God trust you to hold out in the sifting?

Night and day, satan is before God accusing, asking, telling God to prove that you will not curse Him to His face. He is challenging your faithfulness. God may allow him to sift you, because He knows your faith is secured. God knows you will stand on His words. He knows you will endure to the end, so He may allow it. Why is God so confident in this? Because Jesus prayed for you that your faith fails not. His prayer is the fuel to your enduring ability. His prayer is the insurance to any possible damage.

One of the most assuring things is to know Jesus prayed for you before the sifting has started. Even though you are uncertain of what the experience will be like, your faith will not fail you, because Jesus prayed for you.

How is wheat sifted?

It is said to be a process of refinement, a process of filtering and separating-removing lumps and anything unwanted, so as to keep what is important. It is done through thorough examination and screening.

The sifting is not to destroy you but to, among other things, remove some unnecessary things in your life. The devil just comes along to make the sifting experience appear worse, as he tries to thoroughly examine and test you to give up.

When a farmer is sifting wheat manually, the first step is the threshing. Here, the wheat is spread out on the ground and beaten. The next step is to remove the grains by throwing them into the air for the breeze to take away the chaff, then the heavier grains fall back to the ground.

God will allow the sifting because He knows the process won't kill you. After you have been beaten, pressed, shaken, crushed and thrown into the air, let your faith fall back down on God. Do not allow your faith to be blown away in the sifting. The enemy is after the word of God in you, do not let the Word blow away. Hold on to your faith and the promises of God in the sifting.

The devil could only touch the things God instructed him to touch around Job. There is a limit to what you experience in the sifting. This sifting will get rid of the unwanted things on you and in you. Don't miss your greater, focusing too much on the sifting. What the devil meant for evil, the Lord will turn it for your good. Jesus said to Peter:

> *...when thou art converted, strengthen thy brethren. (Luke 22:32b - KJV).*

This is an indication that you will come out alright, with strength enough to strengthen others. Your faith will not fail you and God will not disappoint your faith.

Day 13
Make Room For Your Breakthrough

(Song to listen: Make Room by Jonathan McReynolds)

You don't have enough room to receive what God is about to do. The space is too tight. You are doing and saying too much. You are letting in too much and hearing what everyone has to say.

How can you be asking for the abundance and there is no room to receive it? You are telling God to enlarge your territory and you can't even manage the space you are already in. There is too much happening in your space. Your hands are full with your desires, but you are asking for His will to be done. There is no seed in the ground, but you are asking for rain. You are telling God to open the flood gates of Heaven, but you have no room to receive the outpouring. Moreover, you want the overflow, but you have shut up your bowels of compassion. Let no one stop you from giving; it could be your gift and that is how you make room for your breakthrough: pouring into others for God to pour back into you. Keep making room for your breakthrough.

Go ahead and clean out, empty out, drain out, let out, move out what you need to and make some room for what

God wants to do in your life. God will sometimes show up quicker when you are on empty or on your last, because then you have some room. So, you may think you have nothing, but you have just enough room. When you are down to nothing, He is up to something. When you are empty, He will fill you up.

Some room is needed for the promise to manifest; provision to be made and the way to be seen. Make space for God to step in. Participate in your breakthrough by creating room for the move. You are waiting on God to work it out, but you are fixing it too.

> *Trust in the LORD with all thine heart; and lean not unto thine own understanding. In all thy ways acknowledge him, and he shall direct thy paths. (Proverbs 3:5-6 - KJV).*

Give God some room to intervene and bring justice to the matter. Wait on Him to tell you when to move, for:

> *A man's heart deviseth his way: but the Lord directeth his steps. (Proverbs 16:9 - KJV).*

One of the reasons you have not seen the abundance and overflow that you have been anticipating for a while now, is due to the little room you have given God to work with. Everyone or anyone is your advisor. You called in your neighbours, co-workers, friends, and counsellors into your space. Now you are trying to do what they all suggested. Your breakthrough is now on delay: God has no room in the room. Doubts, feelings, ideologies, and opinions all fill the room. Faith is under pressure; too many doubters are inside. Put them out and make room for God. Jesus had to put them out because they doubted the word of God.

> *After the crowd had been put outside, he went in and took the girl by the hand, and she got up. (Matthew 9:25 - NIV).*

It was after Jesus put them out of the room that the miracle happened. Who is in your room? Do you have a crowd of doubters? They could be holding up your breakthrough. People will come to witness your deliverance but miss it, because God choose to do it when they are gone. Some will only show up to see if the miracle will truly happen. Make room for God, not eyewitnesses and spectators.

God will stop pouring once there is no more room. Elisha asked the widow to go and borrow pots from her neighbours. The moment the son said: "there is no more pots left," the oil stopped flowing. (See 2 Kings 4:3-6). There was no more room, so God stopped pouring. God will only give you what you have the capacity to receive.

Move over something; shift down something; make room for what you have been asking for.

Day 14
You've Won The Fight But Still In The War

(Song to listen: Victory Belongs To Jesus by Todd Dulaney)

> *And from the days of John the Baptist until now the kingdom of heaven suffereth violence, and the violent take it by force. (Matthew 11:12 - KJV).*

The war is not over, even though the victory is already won. There is a bigger picture than what you are seeing before you. The fight may be over, but the war continues.

There is a war for souls, kingdoms, territories and power. Since satan and his angels were thrown out of heaven, he has been raging war in the earth to win souls for his kingdom. He has been raging wars in the hearts of men and turning nations against nations. The war continues until Jesus' return.

It is one battle after the other. The moment you overcome one, there is another to fight. The fight is what you are seeing, the war is behind it influencing the forms it may take in your life. Therefore, you must know what you are up against, in order to know how to stand.

> *For we wrestle not against flesh and blood, but against principalities, against powers, against the rulers of the darkness of this world, against spiritual wickedness in high places. (Ephesians 6:12 - KJV).*

If you don't open your spiritual eyes and see the bigger picture, you will try to escape the fight, expecting the war to end. Each day you have to: "Put on the whole armour of God, that ye may be able to stand against the wiles of the devil." (Ephesians 6:11 - KJV), knowing that the warfare continues, even when the battle is won.

There is a wrestling going on for money, health, power, peace, love, happiness and so much more. Each day comes with another trouble:

> *Man that is born of a woman is of few days and full of trouble. (Job 14:1 - KJV).*

The trouble never goes away forever, once you are in this life.

> *These things I have spoken unto you, that in me ye might have peace. In the world ye shall have tribulation: but be of good cheer; I have overcome the world. (John 16:33 - KJV).*

You can't escape the fight with the mindset that the war will be over. Approach the war with the mindset that you are victorious. This war has been around long before you and will be around long after you are gone.

> *Therefore, since we are surrounded by such a great cloud of witnesses, let us throw off everything that hinders and the sin that so easily entangles. And let us run with perseverance the race marked out for us. (Hebrews 12:1 - NIV).*

Many have passed through it and have overcome what you are now struggling to hold up under. God already has a plan in the war, and He has already given you the victory in the fight, because the battle belongs to Him.

You fight daily battles because you are in a war. This should not be strange to you:

> *Beloved, think it not strange concerning the fiery trial which is to try you, as though some strange thing happened unto you. (1 Peter 4:12 - KJV).*

Your life is not the worst because of the warfare you are experiencing. Many others are under attack too; we are in a war and we have been given all the tools for victory.

> *Stand therefore, having your loins girt about with truth, and having on the breastplate of righteousness; And your feet shod with the preparation of the gospel of peace; Above all, taking the shield of faith, wherewith ye shall be able to quench all the fiery darts of the wicked. And take the helmet of salvation, and the sword of the*

> *Spirit, which is the word of God. (Ephesians 6:14-17 - KJV).*

The temptation won't just come today, but tomorrow you will be tempted too. The weariness and struggles are not just for you but your children's children too. When you win the fight today, you may have to fight again tomorrow and that time it may be a whole new battle.

> *Be sober, be vigilant; because your adversary the devil, as a roaring lion, walketh about, seeking whom he may devour: Whom resist stedfast in the faith, knowing that the same afflictions are accomplished in your brethren that are in the world. But the God of all grace, who hath called us unto his eternal glory by Christ Jesus, after that ye have suffered a while, make you perfect, stablish, strengthen, settle you. (1 Peter 5:8-10 - KJV).*

Each day you step out, you step into a ring. The enemy tries at your strength, faith, peace and joy. The bigger picture is, he is after your soul. Everything won't end in one fight. Just know that God is with you until the end. Prayer is a powerful weapon in the war.

> *Praying always with all prayer and supplication in the Spirit. (Ephesians 6:18a - KJV).*

Even in your sleep, your mind is under attack; your dreams are disturbed. The war is not just a day thing; it happens in the night too. We wrestle, "...against the rulers of the darkness of this world." (See Ephesians 6:12).

You can't escape the fight to escape this war, but you can overcome each battle in this war. There is a bigger thing behind the battles you face daily. Stay in the ring and God will cause the enemies: *"who rise up against you will be defeated before you. They will come at you from one direction but flee from you in seven." (Deuteronomy 28:7b - NIV).*

Day 15
Someone Is Assigned To You

(SONG TO LISTEN: COVER ME BY MARK CONDON)

That person who can build or break you; encourage or discourage you; help or destroy you; get you to soar or cause you to crawl; pray you through or attack you; whether they come with good or bad intentions, someone is assigned to you today. That person could be sent by God as a destiny helper or motivated by the devil to be a destiny slayer. God uses people and so does the devil.

Not everyone is set out to see you go under; there are those who come your way to help you rise. This particular person is on assignment and it is his or her choice who he or she allows to use him or her. There are people close to you today, who the enemy may use to break your confidence, but God will assign another to restore you. While someone is assigned to you, you too are assigned to someone and may become the answer to that person's prayers, if you stay in God's order. What you are about to say, may just be the right words that person needs to hear. You can choose to be a help or an enemy; a dream come true or someone's worst nightmare. The choice rests with you, as to who you allow to use you today.

After the death of Naomi's sons, she had nothing left. So, she decided to go back to her homeland as a bitter and depressed woman. But Ruth, who I believe, was assigned to her, as much as Naomi was assigned to her, decides to stay with her.

> *And Ruth said, Intreat me not to leave thee, or to return from following after thee: for whither thou goest, I will go; and where thou lodgest, I will lodge: thy people shall be my people, and thy God my God: Where thou diest, will I die, and there will I be buried: the LORD do so to me, and more also, if ought but death part thee and me. (Ruth 1:16-17 - KJV).*

There is a destiny helper who is assigned to you. Many of them are struggling to carry out their assignments. Pray your destiny helpers through.

> *...the soul of Jonathan was knit with the soul of David, and Jonathan loved him as his own soul. And Jonathan stripped himself of the robe that was upon him, and gave David, and his garments, even to his sword, and to his bow, and to his girdles. (1 Samuel 18: 1b & 4 - KJV).*

Have you noticed that while Jonathan was assigned to David to deliver him, Saul was on assignment to kill him?

> *...Saul became David's enemy continually. (1 Samuel 18:29b).*

Saul knew the Lord was with David. This is another reason many will assign themselves to you to do good or harm. When they see the hand of the Lord heavily over your life, they will either be against or for you. Instead of encouraging you, they make life difficult for you. But:

> *The angel of the LORD encampeth round about them that fear him, and delivereth them. (Psalm 34:7 - KJV).*

Angels are assigned to you as well.

People are already assigned to invest in your business ideas, dreams, talents and abilities. Pray that they locate you and fulfil their assignments in your life. Likewise, someone somewhere is waiting on your words of strength, your shoulders, your prayers. Each time the Lord assigns someone to you, the devil also assigns someone to you. God's assignment will not return unto Him void, but will accomplish what He sends it to do. There are more with you than those against you, so stand strong today without fear of who may be against you.

Day 16
If He Breaks Your Heart It Is To Save Your Soul

(Song to listen: Sometimes I Cry by Shelly-Ann Watson {or any other version})

Be careful for nothing; but in everything by prayer and supplication with thanksgiving let your requests be made known unto God. And the peace of God, which passeth all understanding, shall keep your hearts and minds through Christ Jesus. (Philippians 4:6-7 - KJV).

You will save yourself the disappointment and heartbreak, if you put it to God and let His peace guard your heart. This emotional roller-coaster has to stop. It is time for emotional peace and stability. You are up and down and all around with your feelings; in and out of relationships and you get attached so easily, making it hard to let go and move on. You would do anything required to keep this one, just so you don't have to start over. You don't really know if this is the will of God for you, but it feels right. Again, you are on to another friendship, job, opportunity and plan. Then later you change your mind about it. Building another thing that God did not approve. Your soul is on the line, but you are in love, passionate and sold-out.

> *For what shall it profit a man, if he shall gain the whole world, and lose his own soul? Or what shall a man give in exchange for his soul? (Mark 8:36-37 - KJV).*

Your soul may be on the line, but you are going ahead with the plans you already have. You may have it all figured out, but because God is the one directing your steps, some things may shift.

> *In their hearts humans plan their course, but the LORD establishes their steps. (Proverbs 16:9 - NIV).*

God has your best interest at heart and as such, He may have to break your heart to save your soul. The compromise is leading to too much dishonour. Now trouble is ahead and you just can't see it, but the God who sees all things is about to detour you, re-route you, slow you down or bring you to a complete stop; just to save your soul.

> *For whom the Lord loveth he chasteneth, and scourgeth every son whom he receiveth. If ye endure chastening, God dealeth with you as with sons; for what son is he whom the father chasteneth not? (Hebrews 12:6-7 - KJV)*

Don't think of it as a punishment. Stand still as God restores you and brings you into emotional peace. You know your emotions are under attack when you are in love with the wrong person, stressed when you should be happy, anxious when you should be patient or free but feeling bound. There are times when you find that you are easily discouraged or distracted by even someone's opinion.

> *Above all else, guard your heart, for everything you do flows from it. (Proverbs 4:23 - NIV).*

Many of the things you are planning to be involved in, or are already in, have never been put to the Lord, because you know He would not approve. He will have to shift your course to save you from insanity, debts, destruction, shame or even death. He is about to even save your reputation. It will hurt for a while, but you learn to bounce back. You will experience the heartache, but you will learn to love again. If you won't surrender, He will cause the situation to change course to lead you right back to His will.

You thought it was the best, but God knew it would be stress. He broke your heart to keep you smiling. It wasn't done God's way, so He is rerouting you. The intention is to save you, before He has to deliver you.

Day 17
Take Your Eyes Off the Enemy

(Song to listen: Only A Look by The Grace Thrillers)

The more you choose to see the enemy, is the less you will see God. The more you focus on the bad, you will never see the good. Your eyes are the gateway to your soul, so be very careful who or what you focus on. If you keep your eyes on what the enemy is doing, you will always doubt the Word of God.

The challenge comes into your life based on where you choose to look, who you choose to see and what you choose to believe.

Take your eyes off the enemy. He knows you are entertaining him, and he will give you things to look at. You don't need to check up on what the enemy is up to for today and what plots and traps are laid out.

> *The angel of the LORD encampeth round about them that fear him, and delivereth them. (Psalm 34:7 - KJV).*

If you choose to watch the enemy's every move today, you will never trust the coverage of God.

> *I will say of the Lord, He is my refuge and my fortress: my God; in him will I trust.*

> *Surely he shall deliver thee from the snare of the fowler, and from the noisome pestilence. He shall cover thee with his feathers, and under his wings shalt thou trust: his truth shall be thy shield and buckler. Thou shalt not be afraid for the terror by night; nor for the arrow that flieth by day; nor for the pestilence that walketh in darkness; nor for the destruction that wasteth at noonday. A thousand shall fall at thy side, and ten thousand at thy right hand; but it shall not come nigh thee. (Psalm 91:2-7 - KJV)*

The more you choose to watch the enemy, is the more distracted you will become. You will see everything that looks hopeless and you will have nothing to rejoice about. The enemy will ensure that you never see God at work. He won't allow you to see that all things are working together for your good. So, you will be more concerned about what is going wrong, what could go wrong and what will go wrong. Since when have you become so negative and doubtful? It could be the day you kept your eyes on the enemy. There are those who believe they must keep an eye on the enemy. Not before long, they start to blame the enemy for everything, when sometimes God has a hand in it, but they can see nothing but enemies around them, plotting destruction against them. Remember, that what you see can affect what you believe.

When the portals of your soul are receptive to the devices of the devil, your desires could change. When he gets into your mind, your meditation and peace of mind is affected.

> *Thou wilt keep him in perfect peace, whose mind is stayed on thee: because he trusteth in thee. (Isaiah 26:3 - KJV).*

Don't allow the enemy to cause you to be miserable, frustrated, angry and anxious about nothing.

> *Be alert and of sober mind. Your enemy the devil prowls around like a roaring lion looking for someone to devour. (1 Peter 5:8 - NIV).*

When he comes in like a flood, the Lord promises to lift up a standard against him. It is not your duty to watch him. Stop exalting his works over the works of the Lord.

When you choose to see God and God alone, your giants become smaller, harmless and fall quicker. I believe that David did not see a giant before him. Everyone else was intimidated by Goliath, but David was quick to challenge him. When your eyes are on the Lord, the greatest thing appears smaller. If all you choose to see is the enemy, everything around you shows up as a giant. Simple situations now start to overwhelm you. Looking to the Lord reduces the size of your giant and changes your perception about them.

When your eyes are on the Lord, you see the good in the worst situations and attitudes of people. Do not allow the enemy to rob you of what God has given you, all because you keep your eyes on him.

> *The thief cometh not, but for to steal, and to kill, and to destroy: I am come that they might have life, and that they might have it more abundantly. (John 10:10 - KJV).*

If you keep your eyes on the Lord, you won't miss your abundant life.

Day 18
Press Some More

(Song to listen: I Am Pressing On by Michael Reid)

...men ought to always pray, and not to faint. (Luke 18:1b - KJV).

And let us not be weary in well doing: for in due season we shall reap, if we faint not. (Galatians 6:9 - KJV).

Many times, you give up praying too quickly. You give up hope, because nothing seems to be changing. Just as God was about to speak, you stopped praying. Right when God was about to respond, you stopped listening, stopped pressing and got up off your knees. The few times you went down in prayer, you thought it should have been enough to get matters changing course. It is about time you press some more.

Jesus took Peter and the two sons of Zebedee with Him to pray. He told them to stay at a point and keep watch with Him. After He prayed and returned, He found them sleeping:

"Couldn't you men keep watch with me for one hour?" he asked Peter. "Watch and

pray so that you will not fall into temptation. The spirit is willing, but the flesh is weak." (Matthew 26:40b-41 - NIV).

Jesus went away to pray a second time and found them sleeping again, because their eyes got heavy. He left them a third time and returned, and He still came back and found them sleeping, so He asked, *"Are you still sleeping and resting?" (See Matthew 26:45)*. As a follower of Christ, many times you fail to press some more with Him. There are many times Jesus finds you asleep in prayer. Whenever the flesh fails, you surrender. You need some persistency and consistency; you can't keep giving up so easily. Press some more.

> *...there was a judge who neither feared God nor cared what people thought. And there was a widow in that town who kept coming to him with the plea, 'Grant me justice against my adversary.' For some time he refused. But finally he said to himself, 'Even though I don't fear God or care what people think, yet because this widow keeps bothering me, I will see that she gets justice...' (Luke 18:2-5 - NIV).*

Likewise, God will bring about justice for His people, *"who cry out to him day and night? Will he keep putting them off? I tell you, he will see that they get justice, and quickly." (See Luke 18: 7-8)*. It may seem long but keep pressing and press some more. Even when it seems like God is not coming through, press some more. Pressing gets you into the presence of God. It gets you to move into realms you would not have gone, if you had nothing to press for. Pressing takes you deeper than where a five-minute prayer can go. When you spend time pressing into the presence of God, you know His voice and He knows yours. The bond is strengthened.

Maybe in this season, God wants you to press some more and that is why the situation is not changing nor the thing moving. The delay is not a denial, it just means you need to press some more. That is the only way the woman with the issue of blood could have made contact with Jesus for her healing. Pressing takes you out for your comfort zone and into the extraordinary. It erupts your faith and determination to receive the impossible.

Daniel mourned, fasted and prayed for twenty-one days for an answer from God. Angels were struggling to get the answer to him, but he was unaware of what the delay was, so he kept on pressing. I believe that Daniel's consistency in prayer helped freed the atmosphere for the angel to get the answer to him *(See Daniel 10)*.

You don't know what or who you are releasing when you press some more. Stay in the presence of the Lord a little while longer and press some more.

> *Ask, and it shall be given you; seek, and ye shall find; knock, and it shall be opened unto you. (Matthew 7:7 - KJV).*

This breakthrough may require some more pressing. You have never gone this deep; you have never prayed like this before. God is calling you higher. Don't stop believing or else you will stop pressing. Put some more pressure on that issue. Stretch your faith a little more and press.

Day 19
Stay The Full Course

(Song to listen: Fully Committed by Kingdom)

Why are you losing the passion already? You just started! Are you starting and stopping again? You are not even halfway into it yet, and you are ready to give up on it! Go all the way! Completing the course is just as important as starting it.

The struggles are real, but don't quit now. The funds are not coming in, your mind is not grasping it, the drive is no longer there, and another opportunity has presented itself. Whatever the excuse is, understand that you did not start on your own. What was your reason for starting in the first place? What did the Lord say? What instruction did you receive? Hold to it and stay the full course, *"Being confident of this, that he who began a good work in you will carry it on to completion until the day of Christ Jesus." (Philippians 1:6 - NIV).*

God is faithful to the promise that is over your life.

> *Does he speak and then not act? Does he promise and not fulfill? (Numbers 23:19b - NIV).*

Do not walk away from the Lord now, when you vowed to go all the way. There are many who left what they started and never got the chance to complete it. Some have lost all desires, others become distracted or delayed by other things. You can miss your set time to transition, because you stopped along the way.

Elisha was following Elijah because he knew his set time would come to transition. So, Elisha stayed the full course with Elijah. Three times Elijah told him to "tarry here" so he can go where the Lord had sent him and Elisha refused.

> ...Elijah said unto him, Tarry, I pray thee, here; for the LORD hath sent me to Jordan. And he said, As the LORD liveth, and as thy soul liveth, I will not leave thee. And they two went on. (2 Kings 2:6 - KJV).

When you know that God will do what He says He will in you, you will stay the full course. Something big is coming and you can sense it. You are confident that God will reward your faithfulness, so you are staying. Elisha stayed because he knew an opportunity would come up for a double anointing.

> And it came to pass, when they were gone over, that Elijah said unto Elisha, ask what I shall do for thee, before I be taken away from thee. And Elisha said, I pray thee, let a double portion of thy spirit be upon me. (2 Kings 2:9 - KJV).

Do not allow anyone to call you down, out or off the course. Stay in the race; stay on track.

> ...the race is not to the swift, nor the battle to the strong... (Ecclesiastes 9:11 - KJV).

It is an endurance race. Stay the full course. Do not leave prematurely, you need the important lessons, experiences and principles of the course in order to matriculate.

Do not jump course because of what you see others achieving in shorter times. Time is not lost waiting on God. You have seen many stop and start again and complete the course, but who tells you it will work for you? **Full course grants full blessing**. You started in faith, so continue in faith. It may seem long, but the end is closer than you think.

Maybe you have started, and the challenges are discouraging and overwhelming. Do not try to escape, when God can help you through it. You may not feel ready right now and you are hardly holding up and balancing well, but stay the full course.

> I have fought a good fight, I have finished my course, I have kept the faith: Henceforth there is laid up for me a crown of righteousness. (2 Timothy 4:7-8a - KJV).

Allow God to complete what He started in you.

Day 20
Can God Trust You?

(Song to listen: Stand by Donnie McClurkin)

Can He trust you with the mountain? Can He trust you to hold out in the valley? In good times and bad, can God trust you to bless Him still? If He puts it on you, if He allows it, if He has a hand in it, can He trust you to still stand?

There are times when you know you are walking upright, and you are confident that God will protect you from all the plots of the enemy. But then, what happens when God allows him to afflict you. What happens when He removes the hedge a little and allow the enemy to carry out his plot against you? Can God trust you then to hold up?

The Lord was confident in Job. He started boasting about Job, even before satan asked about him.

> *And the LORD said unto Satan, Hast thou considered my servant Job, that there is none like him in the earth, a perfect and an upright man, one that feareth God, and escheweth evil? (Job 1:8 - KJV).*

Can you imagine this being the question God is asking the enemy about you? The Lord knows who will fail Him and who will stand faithfully. He knows who to boast about. The Lord knew Job would hold up under pressure. Satan told Him that Job was faithful only because of the hedge that was around his possessions and family.

> *But put forth thine hand now, and touch all that he hath, and he will curse thee to thy face. (Job 1:11 - KJV).*

When God can trust you, He will boast about you. Sometimes when your life experiences an unexpected shift or an unfortunate turn, it could be the Lord boasting about you.

> *And the LORD said unto Satan, Behold, all that he hath is in thy power; only upon himself put not forth thine hand. (Job 1:12a - KJV).*

Job lost all his possessions, children and even his flesh was afflicted. Is this a test of faith or what? In a position like this, you may ask, have I done something wrong? Where is the coverage God promised? Understand that in all this, God permits what you bear and for how long you bear it. He is still in control. He is depending on you to hold up and remain faithful during this test. You can bear it because, His grace is sufficient for you and His strength is made perfect in your weakness. (See 2 Corinthians 12:9).

God could be boasting about you when you got laid off from that job. He could have asked satan this question,

"Have you considered my servant?" Then you start losing some things, because God removed the hedge He had around your possessions. Why you? Simply because He can trust you with trouble. It is one thing after the other; bills start piling up, children are disobedient, financial lack and illnesses. All these things seem to be happening at a time when you were becoming stronger in your spiritual walk and prayer life. Job was so upright that he made sacrifices on behalf of his children in case they had sinned against God. Maybe you too have been praying for your children to ensure they stay in the will of God, but the hedge has been removed and things have gotten worse with your family. After Job got the news, he found strength to worship the Lord in spite of.

> *In all this Job sinned not, nor charged God foolishly. (Job 1:22 - KJV).*

Can God trust you to keep your praise in spite of? Can He trust you to keep your peace, joy and tongue? Job declared, *"Though he slay me, yet will I trust in him: but I will maintain mine own ways before him." (Job 13:15 - KJV).* It may feel as if God is slaying you, but He just trusts you with trouble. The enemy can only go as far as God allows him. Hold on to your integrity. You don't have to curse God and die.

> *For we have not an high priest which cannot be touched with the feeling of our infirmities; but was in all points tempted like as we are, yet without sin. Let us therefore come boldly unto the throne of*

grace, that we may obtain mercy, and find grace to help in time of need. (Hebrews 4:15-16 - KJV).

The process is not forever. The Lord just wants His glory out of your life. He is expecting you to rely on Him to strengthen and lead you through. God will not allow the mission, ministry, task or test to overwhelm you. The Lord has found faithfulness in you, so He is trusting you to hold out until He steps in.

Day 21
Who Am I To You?

(SONG TO LISTEN: YOU ARE GOD BY JERMAINE GORDON)

They replied, "Some say John the Baptist; others say Elijah; and still others, Jeremiah or one of the prophets." "But what about you?" he asked. "Who do you say I am?" (Matthew 16:14-15 - NIV).

If many of you were asked this question, maybe you would start to list the things you hear other people say about Him. You would mention the things you hear in their testimonies, preached about in their sermons or what you read about in the Bible: I hear you are a miracle worker, the saviour of this world, you healed the blind and make the lame walked. Jesus had directed the question in such a way to get a personal response. This question could only be answered out of a personal revelation and relationship that is coined from an intimate place. Who do you say I am? What does your heart know about Me? What is the revelation you got? Who am I to you?

Simon Peter answered, "You are the Messiah, the Son of the living God." Jesus replied, "Blessed are you, Simon son of

> *Jonah, for this was not revealed to you by flesh and blood, but by my Father in heaven." (Matthew 16:16-17 - NIV).*

Who is God to you? Who is He in your situation? Who is He when your back is against the wall and no hope is around? Do you see Him as your Abba (Father/ Daddy), Adonai (Lord), Jehovah Jireh (Provider), Jehovah Rapha (Healer), Alpha and Omega (Beginning and End)?

There are many who have been in the company of Jesus for years and still trust in Him based off the experiences of others. When will you receive your revelation?

The disciples could not cast out the dumb spirit out of a child. Jesus' response was: *"O faithless generation, how long shall I be with you? How long shall I suffer you? Bring him unto me." (Mark 9:19b - KJV).* How could you be walking with Jesus and don't understand the authority you have to cast out demons? Who is He to you? If you don't know Him, you will struggle to trust Him. The revelation comes from a personal place. Are you His sheep or a goat?

> *My sheep hear my voice, and I know them, and they follow me: and I give unto them eternal life; and they shall never perish, neither shall any man pluck them out of my hand. (John 10:27-28 - KJV).*

Many are doing great works in His name and He does not know them, yet they are preaching about Him.

> *Many will say to me in that day, Lord, Lord, have we not prophesied in thy name? and in thy name have cast out devils? And in thy name done many wonderful works? And then will I profess unto them, I never knew you: depart from me, ye that work iniquity. (Matthew 7:22-23 - KJV).*

You can't say you know Him, but He doesn't know you. Have you received your revelation yet? When you know Him, He builds something on you, and He passes authority to you.

> *And Jesus answered and said unto him, Blessed art thou, Simon Barjona: for flesh and blood hath not revealed it unto thee, but my Father which is in heaven. And I say also unto thee, That thou art Peter, and upon this rock I will build my church; and the gates of hell shall not prevail against it. And I will give unto thee the keys of the kingdom of heaven: and whatsoever thou shalt bind on earth shall be bound in heaven: and whatsoever thou shalt loose on earth shall be loosed in heaven. (Matthew 16:17-19 - KJV).*

Who is He to you when doubt steps in? Who is He when you just don't understand?

> *And Moses said unto God, Behold, when I come unto the children of Israel, and shall*

> *say unto them, the God of your fathers hath sent me unto you; and they shall say to me, What is his name? what shall I say unto them? And God said unto Moses, I Am That I Am: and he said, Thus shalt thou say unto the children of Israel, I Am hath sent me unto you. (Exodus 3:13-14 - KJV).*

Leave the revelation to God. He will be to you whoever you want Him to be. If you find yourself struggling to trust His word, then it stems from the relationship you have with Him.

Let's demonstrate:

Ask yourself this question, "Who is God to me?" Shout out about ten descriptive words as quickly as possible, without thinking too hard. If you were able to do it without any delay, then you have something He can build on.

Day 22
It's Not A Mistake But A Design

(Song to listen: My Life Is In Your Hands by Kirk Franklin)

What if it is all a part of God's design for you? What if it is not a mistake but a design? It comes with challenges, struggles, pains and hurts, but it is intended to design your life. Why would the great Architect choose such a design for your life?

You have now started to examine the lives of others around you; comparing yourself. You have tried to be honest, faithful, and obedient to the will of God. Yet, you have been rejected, condemned and abandoned. Could your life be a mistake? Job started to curse the day in which he was born:

> *Let them curse it that curse the day, who are ready to raise up their mourning. Why died I not from the womb? why did I not give up the ghost when I came out of the belly? (Job 3:8,11 - KJV).*

He cursed the day he was born, but *"In all this Job sinned not, nor charged God foolishly."* (Job 1:22 - KJV). Life's struggles may cause you to feel as if your life is a big mistake. But what if it is all a part of God's perfect design for your life? As unfair as it may seem, what if God is working out His perfect design in all of it and this is the path your life must take? I know you may have some suggestions you wish the Lord would take to make your path easier; some persons He could remove and some doors He could open. While a mistake may produce something unwanted, a design will produce something beautiful. Wait on the design to be complete. God has a masterpiece He is working out in your life.

That plaguing health condition make it seem like there is no goodness and mercy following you. You are still waiting to see the purpose behind your pain, to bounce back after the setbacks and to finally win the battle. Just understand that it is all a design, *"And we know that all things work together for good to those who love God, to those who are the called according to His purpose."* (Romans 8:28 - KJV). This is the path your life must take to carry out God's design. Others you are comparing yourself with, have their design to live out. You are a work in progress; never forget that. God is not done with you yet.

The process is a design and God chose your life to fulfil His plan. Don't write yourself off because you think it is a mistake. You belong here, you deserve everything that is good and you will come out victorious. God trusts you to still look good, even in what seems like the worse design, for *"...God is faithful, who will not suffer you to be tempted above that ye are able; but will with the temptation also make a way to escape, that ye may be able to bear it."* (1

Corinthians 10:13 - KJV). No one else could live your life but you.

> *"You did not choose me, but I chose you..."*
> *(John 15:16a - NIV).*

Remain patient, humble and faithful, as God completes your masterpiece look. Job held on throughout an unexpected strange course that God designed for his life, just for His glory to be revealed. A testimony is coming from your experience that will encourage someone else. That is why it is a design; it brings beauty from ashes. Someone will use your life as a point of reference, because you made it. Don't interrupt God's design with your impatience and disobedience. Thanks be to God; He still designs around our faults and setbacks.

What if all you have gone through, all you are going through, or will ever go through, is a part of a divine design for your life? You call it a mistake, misfortune, curse, bad luck or punishment, but God sees a design. What are you showing the world about your process: the mistake or design? Your design is unique to you. The Almighty Architect has a plan to get you out or get you through every situation He allows to cross your path. He has already designed the path you must take to get where He wants you to be. Just stay on the Potter's wheel, as He designs. It will appear as a mistake if you get off the wheel and fix your life your way.

That next test is designed to strengthen you and not to harm you.

But he knows the way that I take; when he has tested me, I will come forth as gold. (Job 23:10 - NIV).

Can God trust you to hold out until He reveals to you what He is working on? **Mistakes have lessons; designs have blessings.**

Day 24
He Will Have To Cover You To Show You

(Song to listen: Cover Me by Mark Condon)

If you are pleased with me, teach me your ways so I may know you and continue to find favor with you. Remember that this nation is your people. And the Lord said to Moses, "I will do the very thing you have asked, because I am pleased with you and I know you by name." Then Moses said, "Now show me your glory." And the Lord said, "I will cause all my goodness to pass in front of you, and I will proclaim my name, the Lord, in your presence. I will have mercy on whom I will have mercy, and I will have compassion on whom I will have compassion." (Exodus 33: 13,17-19 - NIV).

Have you been telling God to show you His glory, that you want to know His ways, to take you higher and deeper in Him and give you revelations? If this is your desire, then He will have to cover you to show you. This is a very powerful experience you are seeking after. I would describe the glory of God as the manifested honour, splendour and beauty of God's holiness. I realize that the more of His glory you see, is the more of His coverage you will need. Moses needed this experience in order to lead God's people. God was willing to show him His glory, but with some requirements:

> *"But," he said, "you cannot see my face, for no one may see me and live." Then the Lord said, "There is a place near me where you may stand on a rock. When my glory passes by, I will put you in a cleft in the rock and cover you with my hand until I have passed by. Then I will remove my hand and you will see my back; but my face must not be seen." (Exodus 33:20-23 - NIV).*

You have been seeking the glory of the Lord, day after day. You want more power and anointing. He will have to cover you to take you there and keep you covered there. He first ensured Moses was standing on a rock. You can't desire God's glory and you are not standing on the solid Rock, Jesus Christ.

> *For in the time of trouble he shall hide me in his pavilion: in the secret of his tabernacle shall he hide me; he shall set me up upon a rock. (Psalm 27:5 - KJV).*

It is a safe foundation to receive the glory that is about to come upon you. The second thing the Lord did while His glory passed by Moses, was to put him in the cleft of the rock and cover him with His hand. When the hand of the

Lord is over you, it comes with complete coverage. To be on the Rock is one thing, but you must also be in the Rock.

> *If ye abide in me, and my words abide in you, ye shall ask what ye will, and it shall be done unto you. (John 15:7 - KJV).*

Coverage must be from all angles.

> *He shall cover thee with his feathers, and under his wings shalt thou trust: his truth shall be thy shield and buckler. (Psalm 91:4 - KJV).*

Also, God said, Moses there will come a time where I will take away my hand and you will get a revelation of Me. The Lord did not show Moses everything, because he would not be able to handle it. The Lord knows how much glory to show you and revelation to give you. David said: *"Such knowledge is too wonderful for me; it is high, I cannot attain unto it." (Psalm 139:6 - KJV).*

His knowledge, righteousness and holiness will consume yours. He will have to cover you to show you. You want to see more, but flesh cannot access it. You have to move into the Spirit for this encounter. The higher you go, the more coverage you will need. The more supernatural encounters you have, you will need to remain covered. When you are seeking more of Him, also seek more of His coverage. I have come to realize that attacks increase when you are exposed to more encounters. You must stay in the Rock to operate effectively. The more He shows you, the more your level of persecution may increase. The warfare may be unique in your life because of what God allows you to be exposed to. It is for your own safety for Him to cover you before He shows you.

Day 25
Internal Struggles Interfere With External Battles

(Song to listen: Surrounded (Fight My Battles) by Leon Timbo)

> *For we wrestle not against flesh and blood, but against principalities, against powers, against the rulers of the darkness of this world, against spiritual wickedness in high places. (Ephesians 6:12 - KJV).*

If you are fighting internal battles, it can affect what is physically standing before you. The warfare on the inside can interfere with the warfare on the outside. Internal things are powerful, because they can give birth to, or destroy, external things.

> *...greater is he that is in you, than he that is in the world. (1 John 4:4 - KJV).*

> *But we have this treasure in earthen vessels, that the excellency of the power may be of God, and not of us. (2 Corinthians 4:7 - KJV).*

> *What goes into someone's mouth does not defile them, but what comes out of their mouth, that is what defiles them. (Matthew 15:11 - NIV).*
>
> *A good man brings good things out of the good stored up in his heart, and an evil man brings evil things out of the evil stored up in his heart. For the mouth speaks what the heart is full of. (Luke 6:45 - NIV).*
>
> *Thy word have I hid in mine heart, that I might not sin against thee. (Psalm 119:11 - KJV).*

Notice, each experience is from internal to external. What you struggle with on the inside can influence how you deal with things externally. Your mindset can affect your actions; it is internal to external. Your internal struggles can affect your battles and cause you to live in defeat. David prayed: *"Create in me a clean heart, O God; and renew a right spirit within me." (Psalm 51:10 - KJV).* David recognized his need for internal cleansing and restoration in order to face what was before him.

You must understand that the wrestling is not against flesh and blood. Whatever is up against you is spiritual and knows what you struggle with. The enemy of your soul knows you are not what you profess to be, but you are fighting external battles. So, when the sons of Sceva went to cast out the evil spirit, the evil spirit answered them and said: *"Jesus I know, and Paul I know, but who are ye?" (Act*

19:15 - KJV). They had to flee for their lives, because the evil spirit leaped on them and they were wounded. Internal struggles can affect external victories. Whatever you are fighting against, knows that you are struggling internally. When your inside is not right with the Lord, your opposers will know, because your fight is not the same.

If you are a limping believer, it will affect how you deal with external battles. Your relationship with people can create more conflicts than resolutions. What is your internal struggle? It could be affecting how you communicate or function effectively in your relationships. Are you struggling with pride, lust, unforgiveness, guilt, fear, hatred, jealousy, and rebellion? Are you struggling with principalities and powers on the inside but trying to fight against them externally?

> *How can Satan cast out Satan? And if a kingdom be divided against itself, that kingdom cannot stand. (Mark 3: 23b-24 - KJV).*

These spirits will keep you bound and losing external battles. Soon, you may find it hard to rebuke the thing you grow to love. If you have no faith, how can you lay hands and see healing take place? If you are struggling with fear, you can't lead anyone. This thing is affecting your confidence, faith, vision and strength. Deal with the inside first.

The Spirit of the Lord chooses to dwell on the inside of you, to give you a lively conscience and teach you all things.

> *But if anybody does sin, we have an advocate with the Father--Jesus Christ, the Righteous One. (1 John 2:1b - NIV).*

Continuous repentance is paramount in all this, in order to bring your heart and mind at the right place to receive instructions from the Lord.

Paul recognized that there was another law at work within him that affected the good he really wanted to do. You have to identify it too, so you can deal with the internal war, in order to fight the external one. You have the spirit of the Lord within to help you overcome the struggles. Do not accept defeat. Work on the internal struggles to experience external victories.

Day 26
Provision Is In The Place Of Your Assignment

(Song to listen: He'll Make A Way by Crabb Family/ Sis. Faith)

Some time later the brook dried up because there had been no rain in the land. Then the word of the Lord came to him: "Go at once to Zarephath in the region of Sidon and stay there. I have directed a widow there to supply you with food." (1 Kings 17:7-9 - NIV).

Your next assignment, mandate, test or step, requires complete faith in God's provision. Jesus said to the disciples: *"...Take nothing for your journey, neither staves, nor scrip, neither bread, neither money; neither have two coats apiece." (Luke 9:3 - KJV).* Where He sends you, He makes provision.

God may just be ready to transition you into what He promised, and you won't see the provision until you move into the place of your assignment. Guess what? You may get there and see nothing there as well; leaving you to be patient, apply faith or even prophecy. There are many who vowed to only move when and if they see the way, the open door or the provision.

Fear and doubt will cause you to sit and question God about the provision, and then hold up the assignment.

> *Now faith is the substance of things hoped for, the evidence of things not seen. (Hebrews 11:1 - KJV).*

God knows that sometimes the only way to get you up from that place, is to dry up things around you that were sustaining you. This will cause you to move into your next assignment by faith. Elijah was instructed to move when the brook dried up. The lack of rain caused his supply to stop flowing. He was now in a different place, on a different mission, with just a word, "I have directed a widow to sustain you." (See 1 King 17:9). Elijah had to trust the Lord and move into the place of his assignment for the provision. However, when he got to the town gate, he found the widow gathering sticks.

> *So he went to Zarephath. When he came to the town gate, a widow was there gathering sticks. He called to her and asked, "Would you bring me a little water in a jar so I may have a drink?" As she was going to get it, he called, "And bring me, please, a piece of bread." "As surely as the Lord your God lives," she replied, "I don't have any bread—only a handful of flour in a jar and a little olive oil in a jug. I am gathering a*

> *few sticks to take home and make a meal for myself and my son, that we may eat it— and die." (1 Kings 17:10-12 - NIV).*

At this point in your place of assignment, maybe you started to question God's word. God, You said You have directed someone to feed me; now I am here, and the person is hungry too. The assignment seems as if it won't go through again or maybe it was not God who really sent me here; there is no provision here. Elijah was not deterred by the widow's desperation. He knew he was on assignment and God already gave him a promise that the widow would sustain him. If and when you get to the place of your assignment and you can't see the provision anywhere, just remember the word of God that He promised to make a way. Therefore, no matter what it looks like, carry on in faith.

> *Elijah said to her, "Don't be afraid. Go home and do as you have said. But first make a small loaf of bread for me from what you have and bring it to me, and then make something for yourself and your son." (1 Kings 17:13 - NIV).*

Declare faith, reinforce the word of God and prophecy over the situation. Elijah assured her: *"For this is what the Lord, the God of Israel, says: 'The jar of flour will not be used up and the jug of oil will not run dry until the day the Lord sends rain on the land.'" (1 Kings 17:14 - NIV).* Sometimes, you may have to end up helping your destiny helpers to help you, when you meet upon them in the place of your assignment. They were directed to help you but need some faith. There are people you will come in contact with along the way that you may have to encourage. Because you are on assignment, everything aligns to your provision. Faith and works must come together in this assignment.

> *She went away and did as Elijah had told her. So there was food every day for Elijah and for the woman and her family. For the jar of flour was not used up and the jug of oil did not run dry, in keeping with the word of the Lord spoken by Elijah. (1 Kings 17: 15-16 - NIV).*

I believe Elijah recognized that the assignment came before the provision. The assignment began with a little provision, just a "handful of flour in a jar and a little olive oil in a jar." (See 1 Kings 17:12). Start the assignment with what you have available; the increase will eventually come. Elijah realized that his assignment was with the widow and she had to be obedient in order for the provision to be seen.

Maybe you have been instructed by God to step out into the place of your assignment. You were told to start it or work on it, but no provision is there, and it requires resources. Do not doubt the ability of God to *"...make a way in the wilderness, and rivers in the desert." (Isaiah 43:19b - KJV).* Your assignment comes with provisions.

Day 27
No Valley
No Mountain

(Song to listen: In The Valley by Martin's Heritage)

For I reckon that the sufferings of this present time are not worthy to be compared with the glory which shall be revealed in us. (Romans 8:18 - KJV).

If we suffer, we shall also reign with him. (2 Timothy 2:12a - KJV)

The valley comes before the mountain.

The battle comes with victory.

Through the trial you will triumph.

The tests perfect your patience.

The valley is next to the mountain. It is ground level, before sky level. Your river Jordan takes you over on the other side. The wilderness came before the Promised Land.

...weeping may stay for the night, but rejoicing comes in the morning. (Psalm 30:5b - NIV).

The mountain needs the valley, as much as the valley needs the mountain.

It is said that the valley is a low area between two hills or mountains; often with a river or stream that runs between them. What is so significant about the valley? There is a stream running through the valley that you won't find on the mountain. A stream to refresh you when the battle gets too hot and your spiritual thirst intensifies. This same stream nourishes the mountain, making it lush and fruitful. It is also said that the fertilizer for the mountain comes from the valley.

It is clear that the valley is sustaining the mountain. No valley, no mountain. Do not despise the valley, it gives a different experience from the mountain. I have spent some time in the valley while hiking in the rural hills of Clarendon, and the valley was my resting place after a long day's journey. The valley is a much cooler place, as it is surrounded by mountains. I observed that the soil in the valley is richer than the soil on the mountain. The soil in the valley is rich enough to grow you. You cannot escape the valley to get on the mountain; you must pass through it.

If you are in the valley, just know that it is not a death sentence.

> *There hath no temptation taken you but such as is common to man: but God is faithful, who will not suffer you to be tempted above that ye are able; but will*

> *with the temptation also make a way to escape, that ye may be able to bear it. (1 Corinthians 10:13 - KJV).*

Many of you may never experience the wealth of the valley because of the mountain mindset you may have. You won't always struggle down there. The valley is for relaxation, peace of mind and restoration too. Every trial that sends you in the valley prepares you for the mountain. Do not allow fear or doubt to overtake you in the valley; you will not die there.

> *Yea, though I walk through the valley of the shadow of death, I will fear no evil: for thou art with me; thy rod and thy staff they comfort me. (Psalm 23:4 - KJV).*

Understand that you must experience the valley before climbing the mountain. Any short cut or escape could be harmful. If you don't learn to climb up on the rough side of the mountain, you may slip and fall back down easily. The rough side of the mountain comes with lumps, bumps, bends, patches and potholes. These are necessary for the best climbing experience. Rough valley experiences make the climb more worthwhile. In case you fall, the bumps and dents will block and stop you from slipping, so you can make a firm grip again. While the smooth side of the mountain makes sliding down very easy, your trials are like the rough side of the mountain that keep you climbing. No valley, no mountain. When you ask God for a mountain, just know that the valley comes with it. Elevation comes with a valley.

Day 28
You May Have To Win

(Song to listen: You Will Win by Jekalyn Carr)

If the Lord tells you that He will strip you down and take away the things that you did not gain in Him, would you see this as a great loss? What about the things that you have gotten so attached to, that are now hindering your worship; would you be devastated by such loss?

God wants you to win again, but this time, it must be in Him. So, He may allow you to lose to some things for your greatest comeback. Your greatest gain is, most times, after your greatest loss. You may have to lose some desires to find yourself back in the will of God. When you are willing to die, you are ready to live. Paul realized that either way, he still wins: *"For to me to live is Christ, and to die is gain."* *(Philippians 1:21 - KJV)*. Understand that if God allows you to lose it, you must look beyond the loss and anticipate the victory that is coming. If you start to view every loss as an opportunity to gain something God's way, you will always experience victories.

If friends have walked away from you, it is not a loss. God could have just pulled you out of what would become a toxic relationship. With God, it is always a victory. **Prepare yourself to lose physically to win spiritually, so you can win again physically.** Let that sink in! The physical loss is preparing you for a spiritual gain. If you take off something, He will put something back on you. Do not fear losing anything when walking with the Lord.

> *Then said Jesus unto his disciples, if any man will come after me, let him deny himself, and take up his cross, and follow me. For whosoever will save his life shall lose it: and whosoever will lose his life for my sake shall find it. (Matthew 16:24-25 - KJV).*

God's love does not tear down but build up. Job knew what it was like to lose in order to win again. He lost everything he owned; one after the other. When his wife realized he was stripped of all that he had, she told him to curse God and die.

> *Dost thou still retain thine integrity? curse God, and die. (Job 2:9b - KJV).*

Job condemned her speech right away:

> *But he said unto her, Thou speakest as one of the foolish women speaketh. What? shall we receive good at the hand of God, and shall we not receive evil? In all this did not Job sin with his lips. (Job 2:10 - KJV).*

I believe in all this Job knew the Lord was too faithful to not have a reward for him after his loss, so he endured to the end. Job received double; the LORD restored his fortunes and gave him twice as much as he had before. (See Job 42:10). Job lost and gained at the hand of God. You cannot lose while serving God. You cannot lose standing on the promises of God. Even when the enemy seems to be robbing you of your joy and peace, you are still victorious. The enemy never wins when God is the one fighting for you. Victory perceived is victory received. Stop counting your losses. There is too much to gain in God for you to look so defeated. Your latter will be greater than the former. **There is too much to gain to lose when you trust God**.

> *Yes, everything else is worthless when compared with the infinite value of knowing Christ Jesus my Lord. For his sake I have discarded everything else, counting it all as garbage, so that I could gain Christ. (Philippians 3:8 - NLT).*

Day 29
The Devil Is Always A Liar

(SONG TO LISTEN: THE ANSWER BY SANDRA BROOKS)

He was a murderer from the beginning, not holding to the truth, for there is no truth in him. When he lies, he speaks his native language, for he is a liar and the father of lies. (John 8:44b - NIV).

The devil will never tell you the truth, even if he wanted to. The truth is not in him. Lies are all he knows to speak.

We often times say, "the devil is a liar" because we can't think of another word to describe his nature. He is an opposer, imitator and deceiver. He tries to change the word and promises of God to distract us from God's truth. This was the first thing he did with Eve in the Garden of Eden. He changed the word of God that Eve received. First, he wanted to hear what God's word says on the matter:

> *Now the serpent was more subtil than any beast of the field which the Lord God had made. And he said unto the woman, Yea, hath God said, Ye shall not eat of every tree*

> *of the garden? And the woman said unto the serpent, We may eat of the fruit of the trees of the garden: but of the fruit of the tree which is in the midst of the garden, God hath said, Ye shall not eat of it, neither shall ye touch it, lest ye die. And the serpent said unto the woman, Ye shall not surely die. (Genesis 3:1-4 - KJV).*

The serpent first asked her about the word God gave to her, then he changed it. Once you tell him what God told you, he will change God's word and cause you to view things from his perspective. Right there, he starts to lie to you. He changed the whole sentence and instruction with a "not": you will "not" surely die. This "not" can change the way you see your life. The devil will say, "you will not live—you will not be healed," then your life takes a hopeless turn. He will change God's word and distort the truth about it:

> *For God doth know that in the day ye eat thereof, then your eyes shall be opened, and ye shall be as gods, knowing good and evil. (Genesis 3:5 - KJV).*

You have to hold on to the word God gave you. The devil will tell you all the things you are missing out on while holding on to God's instruction and soon you may find yourself yielded. The enemy will tickle your fantasies just to get you to desire his lies. When he counteracts the instruction you were given, you may start to see the bad now as good:

> *And when the woman saw that the tree was good for food, and that it was pleasant to the eyes, and a tree to be desired to make one wise, she took of the fruit thereof, and did eat, and gave also unto her husband with her; and he did eat. (Genesis 3:6 - KJV).*

Now, the woman believed and desired the lie over the truth of God, and this led to her yielding to sin. Similarly, this is how you may be pulled away from the truth of God; allowing the enemy to change the word and instruction God gave you. The devil can only tempt; the rest is up to you.

> *But every man is tempted, when he is drawn away of his own lust, and enticed. Then when lust hath conceived, it bringeth forth sin: and sin, when it is finished, bringeth forth death. (James 1:14-15 - KJV).*

You have to remind the devil that he is a liar. Do not stop to listen to what he has to say; you may get caught. It may seem true, but it is a lie. You told him God says you are free, but he tells you generational curses are still over your life. God says you are healed, but the devil reminds you of the pain you are in. When the enemy comes to steal, kill or destroy, he does it through lies. Every time he changes the word of God with a "not," you just declare: you will, it shall be, you are healed, delivered and successful. Don't let him lie to you. Tell him he is a liar.

Day 30
Your Transition Works With Time

(SONG TO LISTEN: YOUR TIME WILL COME BY EDWIN MYERS)

For the vision is yet for an appointed time, but at the end it shall speak, and not lie: though it tarry, wait for it; because it will surely come, it will not tarry. (Habakkuk 2:3 - KJV).

It is going to happen, when it is supposed to happen. In time someone will have to step down for you to step up and step out for you to step in. All of a sudden, the position will be vacant, because you have risen. God sees an Elisha in you and in time, the mantle will be thrown on you.

In time you will be transitioned. Transition speaks to your movement or passage of change from one state, position, stage, place, mindset, level to the next.

The Lord instructed Elijah to anoint Elisha as prophet. Elijah found him with his oxen in the field and passed by him and threw his mantle upon him. Elisha seemed as if he was awaiting such transition; he was ready to move into the call.

> *And he left the oxen, and ran after Elijah, and said, let me, I pray thee, kiss my father and my mother, and then I will follow thee. (1 Kings 19:20a - KJV).*

Your transition works with time, but are you willing to transition when the time comes? When the mantle falls on your back, like Elisha, will you say goodbye to your desires and follow the will of the Lord?

After following Elijah around as his servant and witnessing the power of the Lord upon him, Elisha knew his time would come to transition, because Elijah was supposed to be taken soon. He did not want to let Elijah out of his sight.

> *Then Elijah said to him, "Stay here, Elisha; the Lord has sent me to Jericho." And he replied, "As surely as the Lord lives and as you live, I will not leave you." So they went to Jericho. The company of the prophets at Jericho went up to Elisha and asked him, "Do you know that the Lord is going to take your master from you today?" "Yes, I know," he replied, "so be quiet." (2 Kings 2:4-5 - NIV).*

Elisha knew his time was coming to be transitioned and not even Elijah or the other prophets could have stopped him. So, after a while, both Elisha and Elijah went to Jordan and the time of transition came.

> *When they had crossed, Elijah said to Elisha, "Tell me, what can I do for you before I am taken from you?" "Let me inherit a double portion of your spirit," Elisha replied. "You have asked a difficult thing," Elijah said, "yet if you see me when I am taken from you, it will be yours—otherwise, it will not." (2 Kings 2: 9-10 - NIV).*

Elijah challenged Elisha to stay focused. There are many who want the transition but are not focused or sensitive to the time of the transition. Have you stopped expecting or anticipating to move from where you are? If you take your eyes off the prize, you may miss the time of transition. You must be able to see it before it manifests.

> *Now faith is the substance of things hoped for, the evidence of things not seen. (Hebrews 11:1- KJV).*

In time, you will transition, if you faint not. The seat may be occupied by someone now but keep expecting to move into it. If you are in the valley today, tomorrow you could be on the mountain. **In time, you will move from what was, to what should be; move from what is, to what is to be.**

It won't just be your time, but also your turn. Do not go at it prematurely. You won't have to push anyone out of it either. In time, the shift will happen for the right transition.

For promotion cometh neither from the east, nor from the west, nor from the south. (Psalm 75:6 - KJV).

Look continually to the Lord for instructions. He will tell you when to move. Like Elisha, stay close to it, stay focused to see it, because it works with time.

Day 31
It Will Soon Make Sense

(SONG TO LISTEN: FARTHER ALONG BY GEORGE BANTON)

> *Instead, God chose things the world considers foolish in order to shame those who think they are wise. And he chose things that are powerless to shame those who are powerful. (1 Corinthians 1:27 - NLT).*

You may not understand it now, but you will soon. It hurts, but God will explain it to you later.

> *My brethren, count it all joy when ye fall into divers temptations; knowing this, that the trying of your faith worketh patience. (James 1:2-3 - KJV).*

Those who have passed through it may tell you that it will soon make sense, because it is not a new temptation.

> *There hath no temptation taken you but such as is common to man: but God is faithful, who will not suffer you to be tempted above that ye are able; but will with the temptation also make a way to*

escape, that ye may be able to bear it. (1 Corinthians 10:13 - KJV).

There must be something great coming after all your sufferings:

For I reckon that the sufferings of this present time are not worthy to be compared with the glory which shall be revealed in us. (Romans 8:18 - KJV).

You will know when you should know. God will reveal what is to be revealed:

The secret things belong unto the Lord our God: but those things which are revealed belong unto us. (Deuteronomy 29:29a - KJV).

There are some things that God may allow that really feel unnecessary and unfair. Whatever the Lord allows, He has a purpose and a plan. He has a way of leaving it up to your faith and desperation. If you really want it, then no matter how foolish it looks, you will obey. Sometimes He will choose some unusual ways to deliver you.

And Elisha sent a messenger unto him, saying, Go and wash in Jordan seven times, and thy flesh shall come again to thee, and thou shalt be clean. But Naaman was wroth, and went away, and said, Behold, I thought, He will surely come out to me, and stand, and call on the name of the Lord

> *his God, and strike his hand over the place, and recover the leper. Are not Abana and Pharpar, rivers of Damascus, better than all the waters of Israel? may I not wash in them, and be clean? So he turned and went away in a rage. (2 Kings 5:10-12 - KJV)*

Yes! You wish God would do things the easy, logical and most acceptable way. He won't always move according to your expectation, but you must trust His "foolish" instructions, in order to see the supernatural.

> *When he had thus spoken, he spat on the ground, and made clay of the spittle, and he anointed the eyes of the blind man with the clay, and said unto him, Go, wash in the pool of Siloam, (which is by interpretation, Sent.) He went his way therefore, and washed, and came seeing. (John 9:6-7 - KJV).*

The human mind grapples with the ways of God. We won't always understand why He allows some things to happen or do things a certain way. We look for the sense in all He does and when we can't reason it out, we doubt the hand of God.

> *For my thoughts are not your thoughts, neither are your ways my ways, saith the Lord. For as the heavens are higher than the earth, so are my ways higher than your*

> *ways, and my thoughts than your thoughts. (Isaiah 55:8-9 - KJV).*

You can't always look at things logically, when dealing with a spiritual God.

> *The person without the Spirit does not accept the things that come from the Spirit of God but considers them foolishness, and cannot understand them because they are discerned only through the Spirit. (1 Corinthians 2:14 - NIV)*

When situations come to challenge you, and you can't make sense of it, just trust God. God may want to explain some things to you, but you have shut up your eyes and ears from seeing and hearing and even understanding.

> *Therefore speak I to them in parables: because they seeing see not; and hearing they hear not, neither do they understand. For this people's heart is waxed gross, and their ears are dull of hearing, and their eyes they have closed; lest at any time they should see with their eyes and hear with their ears, and should understand with their heart, and should be converted, and I should heal them. But blessed are your eyes, for they see: and your ears, for they hear. (Matthew 13:13, 15-16 - KJV).*

It won't make sense, if you are not using faith to see. Job said: even though He slay me, yet will I trust Him.

Abraham was told to sacrifice his only son, Isaac, and he obeyed, with the hope of God explaining it to him later. God's "senselessness" may make way for the best opportunity in your life. Give God a chance to explain it to you.

Day 32
Keep Gathering Sticks

(Song to listen: Keep Your Feet On The Ground by Rayon Baugh)

When you are preparing a fire, you may have to gather some sticks. If you gather nothing, you will make nothing. You may not see the provision yet but gather sticks by faith to make the fire. If you prepare your fire, you are expecting the provision. You may be on your last strength but keep gathering what you can; help is on the way.

Elijah got instructions from the Lord to move from the brook and go to a widow, who He had commanded to sustain him.

> *So he arose and went to Zarephath. And when he came to the gate of the city, behold, the widow woman was there gathering of sticks. (1 Kings 17:10a - KJV).*

Elijah found her helping herself, as weak as she was. She was working on making a fire, even with nothing much to put on it. In what state did help find you? Were you gathering sticks or begging bread? Were you trusting God to make a way while you do your part?

Gathering sticks could mean: making something out of nothing, living on your last, doing your part or enduring a process. In this case, the widow was living on her last. From my understanding, when you gather sticks to make a fire, it means you have nothing much preparing. When you gather wood, your pots should be bigger and contain more. This widow's last was not much, because she was found gathering sticks. Some people may see you in the supermarket shopping at times and don't even know that you are just there gathering sticks; what you gather is all you could afford. Electric and gas stoves are prevalent, but they found you gathering sticks.

When the prophet showed up, he saw the state of the woman, but still asked for water and bread. It is a test of faith to give from nothing and that is the time people tend to ask. A good woman likes to have food in her house to entertain strangers. She will try to make something of what she has to ensure a stranger is well accommodated. Elijah left this widow no choice but to pour out to him.

> *And she said, As the Lord thy God liveth, I have not a cake, but an handful of meal in a barrel, and a little oil in a cruse: and, behold, I am gathering two sticks, that I may go in and dress it for me and my son, that we may eat it, and die. (1 Kings 17:12 - KJV).*

She was more willing to go for the water for Elijah, than her last bread. Elijah came as her help, and she was about to find out.

> *And Elijah said unto her, Fear not; go and do as thou hast said: but make me thereof a little cake first, and bring it unto me, and after make for thee and for thy son. For thus saith the Lord God of Israel, The barrel of meal shall not waste, neither shall the cruse of oil fail, until the day that the Lord sendeth rain upon the earth. (1 Kings 17: 13-14 - KJV).*

Her days of gathering sticks were over, through her obedience and faith in the word of God. She had a meal to eat every day since then.

You may have been gathering sticks for a while now, but no help has come yet and things are still the same. Help is on the way; keep gathering what you can and prepare your fire.

> *I was young and now I am old, yet I have never seen the righteous forsaken or their children begging bread. (Psalm 37:25 - NIV).*

The Lord has assured you that, "*My grace is sufficient for thee: for my strength is made perfect in weakness.*" (See 2 Corinthians 12:9).

Abraham gathered wood to sacrifice his son. This was a great sacrifice, but he endured by faith and the Lord provided a ram to sacrifice instead. God is about to put something on your fire. Gather your sticks in faith and obedience. Do not complain and murmur but give thanks in all things. Keep giving out of nothing. Keep applying for it. Keep saving towards it. Keep gathering your sticks. Help is on the way to you.

Day 33
No Purpose No Peace

(Song to listen: Peace In My Soul by Jermaine Edwards)

I believe it is hard to identify and walk in your purpose, without first accepting and knowing Christ Jesus as your Lord and personal Saviour. What you are pursuing could be passions and plans.

> *Many are the plans in a person's heart, but it is the Lord's purpose that prevails. (Proverbs 19:21 - NIV).*

> *In their hearts humans plan their course, but the Lord establishes their steps. (Proverbs 16:9 - NIV).*

It is a peaceful experience knowing who you are in Christ Jesus and what He had in mind for you to carry out when He formed you in your mother's womb.

> *Before I formed you in the womb I knew you, before you were born I set you apart; I appointed you as a prophet to the nations. (Jeremiah 1:5 - NIV).*

No matter where Jeremiah went or what he did, this purpose was upon him to be fulfilled.

> *But I have raised you up for this very purpose, that I might show you my power and that my name might be proclaimed in all the earth. (Exodus 9:16 - NIV).*
>
> *For it is God who works in you to will and to act in order to fulfill his good purpose. (Philippians 2:13 - NIV).*

Being without purpose makes life meaningless and restless. You face circumstances not knowing why and if it was good for you.

> *And we know that in all things God works for the good of those who love him, who have been called according to his purpose. (Romans 8:28 - NIV).*

When you are walking in purpose, every situation you find yourself in has a lesson. Each encounter has a meaning and life is never looked at the same way.

Purpose, based on my understanding, is that God-given mandate that is set over your life to impact the kingdom of God. Lives will be transformed through it and your life will be meaningful with it.

There is a mandate with your name on it. That is where your peace is, the will of God is and freedom is experienced. Are you walking in your divine purpose or are you still seeking to know what it is? You must desire to know what God requires of you; why He keeps calling your name every morning. It could not be just to go to work, get married, raise a family and pay bills. What is the purpose of His interest in you? The closer you get to finding the answers to these questions, the more at peace your mind will be. Living outside your purpose can be a frustrating experience, because no matter what you achieve, there is a void that still lingers and only God's purpose for you can fill it.

An unfulfilled purpose, leads to an unfulfilled life. There is something missing; something that you have not done yet. The degrees are there, a good job is on the list, business, and many other accomplishments. Peace resides in purpose. Once you walk out of purpose, you walk out of the will and liberty of God.

Jonah disobediently fled on a boat to Tarshish, to avoid carrying out the will of God. His life took a destructive turn when he stepped out of his purpose. When the storm arose at sea, the men had to throw him overboard for peace to return on the sea. (See Jonah 1:1-15). When you flee from purpose, trouble follows you. You may create a storm everywhere you go. Jonah accepted his purpose in the belly of the fish.

How many times will life have to throw you overboard for you to stay in the will of God and walk in purpose? How many times will the situation have to swallow you up for you to refocus? It is time for God to be glorified and the desires of flesh to be put off. It is not purpose, if God gets no glory out of it. Think about it, if you die without fulfilling the purpose of God over your life, then your living was in vain. If you are confused about it, you may find yourself trying to live out another man's calling.

Start to align yourself with God, so He can show you where you must be. It is time for your life to be more fulfilling; it is time for purpose to be answered; it is time for you to be at peace with yourself.

Day 34
Persistence Breaks Resistance

(SONG TO LISTEN: CAN'T GIVE UP NOW BY MARY MARY)

The Lord instructed the army to march around the city of Jericho SEVEN TIMES for the wall to come down. The first day they got up early and marched around the city once, while the seven priests marched with them and blew their trumpets. At this time, they may have been booming with excitement. The second day they marched around the city once and returned to the camp. The excitement may have still been there. The fourth day they went around the city once and returned to the camp. Maybe here, they started to push and press their way. The fifth day they marched once and returned to the camp again. Why is nothing shaking or shifting yet, they may have thought. The sixth day they did it again. The march may have gotten slower by this time and faith wavering, but they still went out on the seventh day. On this day, they marched around the city seven times, this required more pressing, pushing, marching and then shouting. On the seventh lap, the priests blew the trumpet and the army shouted at Joshua's command and the wall collapsed. (See Joshua 6:1-20).

To march once per day must have seemed like a waste of time, but it is not how many times you do it within a day, it is your overall consistency in doing it. If you go at it one day at a time, the Lord will give you strength each day. It is not how many times you hit the spot, but how persistently and obediently you do it. Something will break eventually. Through persistence, miracles come. Your determined faith can break any resistance.

A woman pressed her way to Jesus, to break a stubborn blood issue she had been struggling with for twelve years. This issue had her going from doctor to doctor, and none could help. Her persistence broke through the thick crowd for a single touch of Jesus' garment. She was determined to make contact and eventually she did, drying up her stubborn bleeding problem.

They told blind Bartimaeus to keep silent, as he tried repeatedly to get Jesus' attention.

> *Many rebuked him and told him to be quiet, but he shouted all the more, "Son of David, have mercy on me!" Jesus stopped and said, "Call him." So they called to the blind man, "Cheer up! On your feet! He's calling you." (Mark 10:48-49 - NIV).*

Persistence can break the resistance over your breakthrough. Some of the miracles you are expecting will only come through consistently praying, fasting and applying the word of God over them. When you are persistent, you find yourself continuing in faith, in spite of the difficulty you face or the opposition around you. Some walls, giants, and situations will put up a resistance, but stand determined to win. Not everything will comply with you. There are some illnesses, conditions, giants that will put of a fight. Don't give up too quickly. Press some more, pray some more, be a little more disciplined. Remain persistent, in spite of the resistance.

When you experience repeated resistance, it may discourage you from making more attempts. When the opposition becomes harder to break or penetrate, you may feel tempted to give up. Most times you ignore the thing when it was just a small matter and now it has become like a giant before you. So, it is unbearable for you at that stage, but even giants fall. The longer you wait, the stronger some things may become, and the more energy it may require from you. The moment you see it form, go at it. Even when signs and symptoms return, do not let up.

Some situations have been a part of your life for years, and you have done all you can, but nothing has changed. You have declared deliverance and claimed your healing, but it is still there like a thorn in your flesh. Your persistence will break that resistance. This condition or situation that stands strong before you just won't break down and fall. Could it be that you only have faith for today, but not the other days? Understand, the army went around the wall once per day for seven days. Get persistent and *"Pray without ceasing." (1 Thessalonians 5:17 - KJV).*

> *Praying always with all prayer and supplication in the Spirit. (Ephesians 6:18a - KJV).*

> *And let us not be weary in well doing: for in due season we shall reap, if we faint not. (Galatians 6:9 - KJV).*

The grace of God is sufficient to keep you in your persistence, and His strength will be made strong when you get weak. (See 2 Corinthians 12:9).

> *Ask, and it shall be given; seek, and he shall find; knock, and it shall be opened unto you. (Matthew 7:7 - KJV).*

Something is about to break.

Day 35
You Are In It To Come Out

(SONG TO LISTEN: THE SUN WILL SHINE AGAIN BY JUDITH GAYLE)

Why have you started making your bed where you should not be resting? You are now expecting what is not your expected end; accepting, settling, with a life of trouble.

You are only going through that process to come out of it. Don't stay there longer than the expected time, making a temporary thing, permanent. It must pass over you; troubles don't last always. Experiences are time bound, so your season must change.

> *To everything there is a season, and a time to every purpose under the heaven. (Ecclesiastes 3:1 - KJV).*

You are in it to come through it and out of it.

> *For his anger endureth but a moment; in his favour is life: weeping may endure for a night, but joy cometh in the morning. (Psalm 30:5 - KJV).*

You must go through the darkness of the night to experience the dawn of a new day. Be careful how you are becoming adjusted to the troubles in your life.

> *Humble yourselves therefore under the mighty hand of God, that he may exalt you in due time. (1 Peter 5:6 - KJV).*

There is a period of restoration and elevation.

> *But the God of all grace, who hath called us unto his eternal glory by Christ Jesus, after that ye have suffered a while, make you perfect, stablish, strengthen, settle you. (1 Peter 5:10 - KJV).*

You will pass through it or it will pass over you soon. As challenging as it is, you are in this one to come out.

> *My brethren, count it all joy when ye fall into divers temptations; knowing this, that the trying of your faith worketh patience. (James 1:2-3 - KJV).*

You will learn some vital things through it, but your time of transition will come. God could be working on your patience, character and heart, which is why you are still going through what you are going through. You are begging to come out of it, but He sees a training ground for you.

> *And the Lord said, Simon, Simon, behold, Satan hath desired to have you, that he may sift you as wheat: but I have prayed for*

> *thee, that thy faith fail not: and when thou art converted, strengthen thy brethren. (Luke 22:31-32 - KJV).*

Jesus knew that though the devil would sift Peter, he will come out strengthened. He already secured Peter's deliverance through prayer. I believe Job knew he was coming out as well. He knew this was not his final destination. So, he held on to the word of God, even in the face of ridicule.

The reason we become so frustrated in the process of waiting to come out, is because God is working in His own time. He may not deliver you from it right away when you call on Him. Your frustration intensifies when you start to expect God to work things out according to your will and time. When this does not happen, you start to plan your life around the situation. You choose to see nothing beyond what you are faced with.

You start to accept life just the way it is. When the children of Israel could not reach the Promised Land in their time, they started to murmur and complain, then eventually became rebellious. They despised the wilderness, as it seemed never-ending. But because the Lord gave them a promise, they were in it to come out.

Joseph found himself in Egypt; sold, accused and imprisoned, but he was in it to come out of it. The cupbearer forgot him in prison, after he begged him to mention his name to Pharaoh. When you are in it, many may forget you, but you will come through. His gift opened a room for him, and he became the Governor of Egypt (See Genesis 39-41). The Lord will even create a situation just to pull you out. They forgot you, but He will cause them to remember you.

Keep learning and growing in it, you will soon come out. If the troubles do not pass you, God will cause you to journey pass them. It is just a path you must take and you will move on to newer testimonies and encounters along the way. Don't seek out any escape route, go through it humbly. If you don't go through this, you may have to pass this way again.

Come on! Don't get adjusted; don't become attached to your current state and die there. You are coming out!

Day 36
Who Authorized You To Surrender?

(Song to listen: Can't Give Up Now by Mary Mary)

The story is told of a Japanese soldier, Hiroo Onoda, who for twenty-nine years after World War II, continued to hide, fight and kill in the jungles of the Philippines, all because he did not believe the war was over. He finally surrendered, when his former commanding officer was flown in to see him and revoked the original order in person. Hiroo Onoda said he was ordered not to surrender by his commanding officer, and he obeyed, even when he was the last man standing. The BBC says, Mr. Onoda ignored several attempts made before to get him to surrender.[2]

Who told you to surrender? Who authorized you to give up? Did your situation, conscience, family, friends, enemies or your Commanding Chief, Jesus Christ, command you to surrender? Were you too frustrated, impatient or burdened?

When you are in a battle or situation that is overwhelming to the breaking point, who do you look to for

---
[2] bbc.com/news/world-asia

authorization? When you can't take it anymore and you just can't produce the faith required to fight on, whose command do you listen for? Too many trained soldiers are surrendering without God's authorization.

> *I have fought the good fight, I have finished the race, I have kept the faith. Now there is in store for me the crown of righteousness, which the Lord, the righteous Judge, will award to me on that day—and not only to me, but also to all who have longed for his appearing. (2 Timothy 4:7-8 - NIV).*

> *Fight the good fight of the faith. Take hold of the eternal life to which you were called when you made your good confession in the presence of many witnesses. (1 Timothy 6:12 - NIV).*

Many have quit the race for another prize.

> *Do you not know that in a race all the runners run, but only one gets the prize? Run in such a way as to get the prize. Everyone who competes in the games goes into strict training. They do it to get a crown that will not last, but we do it to get a crown that will last forever. (1 Corinthians 9:24-25 - NIV).*

Job loved his wife, but she could not authorize him to surrender. When she told him to curse God and die, he answered her as faithfully as he could.

> *His wife said to him, "Are you still maintaining your integrity? Curse God and die!" He replied, "You are talking like a foolish woman. Shall we accept good from God, and not trouble?" In all this, Job did not sin in what he said. (Job 2:9-10 - NIV).*

There are people who will try their best to get you to give up along the way; on the battlefield or on your goals. As a true soldier, you must know the Lord is with you and He has the final say over your life.

The Lord did not want Jehoshaphat and his army to go to war and surrender, so He told them the battle belongs to Him.

> *You will not have to fight this battle. Take up your positions; stand firm and see the deliverance the Lord will give you, Judah and Jerusalem. Do not be afraid; do not be discouraged. Go out to face them tomorrow, and the Lord will be with you. (2 Chronicles 20:17 - NIV).*

Who told you to fall defeated, to lie down and die or step out of the ring? You want to give up on the children, relationship, ministry, job or even yourself. A faithful soldier fights to the end, until he is told otherwise. No retreat; no surrender! This is not a speed race, it is an endurance race. Just get to the finish, *"Looking unto Jesus the author and finisher of your faith." (Hebrews 12:2a - KJV).* Do not surrender without an authorization from God. You will be left too vulnerable to the enemy. Get approval first. The enemy knows who is approved by God and who is not, because he looks for the mark of authorization upon you. If God has authorized you to live, then who can take your life?

> *No weapon that is formed against thee shall prosper; and every tongue that shall rise against thee in judgment thou shalt condemn. This is the heritage of the servants of the Lord, and their righteousness is of me, saith the Lord. (Isaiah 54:17 - KJV).*

> *The thief cometh not, but for to steal, and to kill, and to destroy: I am come that they might have life, and that they might have it more abundantly. (John 10:10 - KJV).*

Get back on the track and run the race; get back in the ring and fight on, your authorization comes with power.

> *Behold, I give unto you power to tread on serpents and scorpions, and over all the power of the enemy: and nothing shall by any means hurt you. (Luke 10:19 - KJV).*

It is not over; you still have the victory.

Day 37
The Devil Doesn't Want What You Have

(Song to listen: Still Have Joy by Ron Kenoly)

The thief cometh not, but for to steal, and to kill, and to destroy. (John 10:10a - KJV).

If he steals it, it is not to keep it; the next step is to kill and destroy.

The enemy just doesn't want you to have it. If you lose what God gave to you, then killing and destroying you will be easy. Understand this, what you have won't benefit the devil, but if he robs you of it, you will not benefit from it. He doesn't rob your peace because he wants it, he just wants you to be frustrated, anxious and confused. He is not after your joy, hope and salvation because he could do well with them. His aim is to slowly destroy you. The devil is already doomed and there is no future for him. So, he will try to take as many with him on that path of hopelessness.

Some people will oppress you because they can. Your possessions do not intimidate them, they just do not want to see you flourishing. The Lord left the Israelites in the hands of an oppressive set of people, the Midianites, for seven years. The Israelites had to hide in mountain clefts, caves and strongholds, as the oppression was overwhelming for them:

> *Whenever the Israelites planted their crops, the Midianites, Amalekites and other eastern peoples invaded the country. They camped on the land and ruined the crops all the way to Gaza and did not spare a living thing for Israel, neither sheep nor cattle nor donkeys. They came up with their livestock and their tents like swarms of locusts. It was impossible to count them or their camels; they invaded the land to ravage it. Midian so impoverished the Israelites that they cried out to the Lord for help. (Judges 6:3-6 - NIV).*

The Midianites never seemed to have a real reason for oppressing the Israelites. They never took what the Israelites had, they just killed and destroyed. They camped out on the land, just to ensure that the Israelites saved nothing. The enemy doesn't want what you have, the oppression is to destroy you. The Israelites cried out to the Lord and He assured them through a prophet:

> *I brought you up out of Egypt, out of the land of slavery. I rescued you from the hand of the Egyptians. And I delivered you from the hand of all your oppressors; I drove them out before you and gave you their land. (Judges 6:8b-9 - NIV).*

The enemy wants to see you poor and helpless, but your God will not allow that. He will supply your needs and restore what you have lost.

> *And I will restore to you the years that the locust hath eaten, the cankerworm, and the caterpiller, and the palmerworm, my great army which I sent among you. (Joel 2:25 - KJV).*

What the devil doesn't know is that your joy is not connected to your possessions and material things. So, when he destroys, you are still smiling and praising God. When Job lost his children and possessions, he tore his robe, shaved his head and fell to the ground in worship. (See Job 1:20).

Keep your praise, joy and peace of mind. The Lord will not allow you to perish under the enemy's oppression. He has already made a way of escape or a way for you to endure it.

> *There hath no temptation taken you but such as is common to man: but God is faithful, who will not suffer you to be tempted above that ye are able; but will with the temptation also make a way to escape, that ye may be able to bear it. (1 Corinthians 10:13 - KJV).*

The enemy will be around to see the Lord prepare a table before you in his presence; God will anoint you and your cup will run over. Goodness and mercy will hunt you down and you shall remain in the house of the Lord for ever. (See Psalm 23:5-6). The enemy can steal, kill and destroy all he wants, but the Lord gives abundant life (See John 10:10). You will bounce back from your setback; your opposer will grow weary and your restoration will come.

Day 38
Love Them Still

(SONG TO LISTEN: GOD FAVORED ME BY HEZEKIAH WALKER)

Love is a language stronger than hate.
Love is forgiveness; it doesn't run away.
Love needs no weapon; it is its own defence.
In the end, love will always win.³

The disciples asked:

> *Master, which is the great commandment in the law? Jesus said unto him, thou shalt love the Lord thy God with all thy heart, and with all thy soul, and with all thy mind. This is the first and great commandment. And the second is like unto it, thou shalt love thy neighbour as thyself. On these two commandments hang all the law and the prophets. (Matthew 22:36-40 - KJV).*

You may ask, what if they plot evil against me, Lord? I am sure He would tell you to love them still.

---

³ Travis Greene- Love Will Always Win

> *But I say unto you, Love your enemies, bless them that curse you, do good to them that hate you, and pray for them which despitefully use you, and persecute you. (Matthew 5:44 - KJV).*

The Lord's way of showing love is different from what the world demonstrates. The world says hate those who hate you and love those who love you. But the word of God says:

> *Love your enemies, do good to those who hate you, bless those who curse you, pray for those who mistreat you. If someone slaps you on one cheek, turn to them the other also. If someone takes your coat, do not withhold your shirt from them. Give to everyone who asks you, and if anyone takes what belongs to you, do not demand it back. Do to others as you would have them do to you. If you love those who love you, what credit is that to you? Even sinners love those who love them. And if you do good to those who are good to you, what credit is that to you? Even sinners do that. (Luke 6:27-33 - NIV).*

Learn to love in spite of. Look to God for His grace to help you to love them still. You live, work and worship with them; they don't deserve it but love them still. In doing this, goodness, favour, grace and mercy will follow you.

> *Love is patient, love is kind. It does not envy, it does not boast, it is not proud. It does not dishonor others, it is not self-seeking, it is not easily angered, it keeps no record of wrongs. Love does not delight in evil but rejoices with the truth. It always protects, always trusts, always hopes, always perseveres. (1 Corinthians 13:4-7 - NIV).*

Can you love like this? The love of God in you can help you. The love demonstrated to you by God will strengthen you. It is a difficult thing to be neglected, mistreated and accused by your own, and find the strength to still love them.

> *Though my father and mother forsake me, the Lord will receive me. (Psalm 27:10 - NIV).*

God leaves you with no excuse, but to love them still. It was an act of love that caused Jesus to be nailed to a cross that He did not deserve.

> *For God so loved the world, that he gave his only begotten Son, that whosoever believeth in him should not perish, but have everlasting life. (John 3:16 - KJV).*

It was love that caused Christ to die for us, while we were sinners. Love can cause you to do some unbelievable things: it has that power and influence. Love can cause a person's behaviour to change toward you. Love is a weapon with its own defence. It is a transformation tool. Love over hate, abuse and punishment, can be far more effective.

I can understand that they don't deserve it, but try it; love them still. Forgive them and let nothing but love flow out of you. If you should examine the number of times you stretched and took advantage of the love of God, but He can't help but to love you still.

After Jacob deceived Esau of his birth right and tricked his father into blessing him instead, he fled from home. There was no sympathy from his brother. He left Esau with nothing. However, after leaving home, years later he had to pass that way again and had to meet up on his brother, Esau. However, when he remembered what he did, he feared his brother would try to kill him. There was a great tension and a battle plan, when they were finally about to meet. Unexpectedly, when Esau saw his brother, he greeted him with a hug and a kiss. (See Genesis 32 & 33). All the bitterness, rage and uncertainties went, in one embrace.

You may have to pass that way again; you may meet those same people again. Ensure you always deal with individuals you come across in love, so the favour of God can go before you. Remember this: love always wins. They deserve otherwise, but don't treat them as their sins deserve, show them love instead. Let the enemy be shocked at how you handled the situation. Love can win this battle. Now go in love.

Day 39
What You're Feeding Is Growing

(SONG TO LISTEN: CHANGE ME BY TAMELA MANN)

Whatever you are feeding, you are giving life to it. You are giving it an opportunity and a space to grow and thrive. It is not that big of a deal, but you are giving it more attention than it deserves. You are feeding something that was not meant to grow. It is shooting off quickly and you can no longer control it.

Here is a principle from the word of God: once the earth remains, there will be seedtime and harvest; anything you plant will grow and bear fruit (See Genesis 8:22). Be careful what you plant inside your mind or heart; it will grow. Also, be very careful of what is attaching itself to you to thrive. It will only survive and grow, if you keep feeding it. If you are not quick to repent or forgive, check what is growing inside you. Refuse certain seeds that are destined to bear corrupt fruits. The things you see surviving could be caused by your unintentional nurturing. From time to time, you may find that you become an emotional hoarder; holding on to everything that caused you pain, hurt, grief, sadness, shame, discomfort and guilt. On the right day, you find the right music to listen so you can cry in self-pity; feeding emotions that should not grow.

If you are feeding your past, there will be no room for your future to thrive; one will outgrow the other. Anything, good or bad you plant and feed, you have to expect growth. Here is another principle from the word of God:

> *Be not deceived; God is not mocked: for whatsoever a man soweth, that shall he also reap. For he that soweth to his flesh shall of the flesh reap corruption; but he that soweth to the Spirit shall of the Spirit reap life everlasting. And let us not be weary in well doing: for in due season we shall reap, if we faint not. (Galatians 6:7-9 - KJV).*

There are some traditional seeds you should not be feeding the next generation. It never impacted your life, but you want to pass it on. There are some seeds you know will not bring benefit to your life, but you allow them to fall on your good ground. Some seeds should be devoured the moment they are thrown on your good ground. There are those you should allow the word of God to choke; seeds that should not touch your soil at all, for growth to happen.

> *And when he sowed, some seeds fell by the way side, and the fowls came and devoured them up: some fell upon stony places, where they had not much earth: and*

> *forthwith they sprung up, because they had no deepness of earth: and when the sun was up, they were scorched; and because they had no root, they withered away. And some fell among thorns; and the thorns sprung up, and choked them: but other fell into good ground, and brought forth fruit, some an hundredfold, some sixtyfold, some thirtyfold. (Matthew 13: 4-8 - KJV).*

When people speak some negative things over you, instantly scorch, devour and choke those words with the word of God. The moment you are reminded of the hurts, do not let it fall on your good soil. Do not be the bearer of the wrong seed. If you speak positively or negatively repeatedly, you sow a seed into your life. Be sober about what you are accepting and allowing to grow. Anything that can grow, will grow. The longer you take to dig up the seed, the stronger its rooted. Don't let it pass seed-stage to tree-stage; it may take more work to cut it down.

Don't feed that fear, negative feeling or word. You may struggle to chop down the tree of unforgiveness, resentment and fear. The tree may bear fruit and end up feeding your children. Soon, they love only the people you love and hate the people you hate. Many parents are struggling to be effective because of seeds of bitterness on the inside. If what you are bearing is not the fruit of the spirit: "love, joy, peace, longsuffering, gentleness, goodness, faith, meekness, temperance" (See Galatians 5:22-23), then cut it down. The sun is about to go down,

"...let not the sun go down upon your wrath" (Ephesians 4:26b - KJV). Do not feed another bad seed. Make it right before it grows and gets out of control.

Day 40
God Won't Bless That Mess

(Song to listen: Bless Me by Donald Lawrence/Tri-City Singers)

No matter how beautiful it looks; no matter how perfect it seems; no matter how right you think it is; no matter how decorated you make it appear to be, it is still going against the will of God; still a dishonour to Him.

The Lord has been directing you from that decision you want to make. Time and time again, He sends His word with confirmations to you on it. If it is not in His will, He won't bless it. He is saving you from yourself and that danger ahead.

If you decide to still go ahead with it, it will turn into a mess. His grace and mercy will undoubtedly be extended to you though, because He is not a God to forsake His own. But it will be challenging, as you would now be doing things on your own. Here, you will be exposed to the deception of the enemy without much coverage, and this may complicate things for you. At first, it may seem right, but it will change course because God is not in it. Please guard yourself from the impending deception, compromise, discouragement and isolation.

> *There is a way which seemeth right unto a man, but the end thereof are the ways of death. (Proverbs 14:12 - KJV).*

God may have been silent on the matter for a while now, to observe your obedience to His word. God has already given you clear instructions, but your desires are confirming something else.

If your prayers are for the downfall of another, don't even seek God's blessing or approval on it.

> *If I regard iniquity in my heart, the Lord will not hear me. (Psalm 66:18 - KJV).*

It doesn't matter who you are and the position you hold, God won't bless your mess. **The wages of sin is still death.** (See Romans 6:23). You already know it is a complete dishonour to God and you expect Him to change His word to approve you. Understand that God exalts His word above His name. (See Psalm 138:2). If you go against His word, you dishonour Him, and the thing immediately becomes a mess.

The Lord sent Nathan with a word to David, after He messed up:

> *Then Nathan said to David, "You are the man! This is what the Lord, the God of Israel, says: 'I anointed you king over Israel, and I delivered you from the hand of*

> Saul. I gave your master's house to you, and your master's wives into your arms. I gave you all Israel and Judah. And if all this had been too little, I would have given you even more. Why did you despise the word of the Lord by doing what is evil in his eyes? You struck down Uriah the Hittite with the sword and took his wife to be your own. You killed him with the sword of the Ammonites. Now, therefore, the sword will never depart from your house, because you despised me and took the wife of Uriah the Hittite to be your own.'" (2 Samuel 12:7-10 - NIV).

God will not be silent for long. He will speak. If you continue in the mess, you will not enjoy the benefits of His perfect plans for you. Put a stop to the mess before God does. Save yourself the disappointment. What you are trying to hold on to may seem good, but God has something better. Let go of the mess and hold on to the blessing.

What do you have before you, awaiting a decision? What step do you want to take that seems compromising? It is okay to walk away, if God does not approve it. It has great opportunities and benefits, but it is not God-approved. It will get messy in your hands. God can keep you from falling, let Him.

> And he said unto me, My grace is sufficient for thee: for my strength is made perfect in

weakness. Most gladly therefore will I rather glory in my infirmities, that the power of Christ may rest upon me. (2 Corinthians 12:9 - KJV).

He has great plans ahead for you. Let go of the mess.

"For I know the plans I have for you," declares the Lord, "plans to prosper you and not to harm you, plans to give you hope and a future." (Jeremiah 29:11 - NIV).

Day 41
Where You Sow You May Not Reap

(SONG TO LISTEN: SOW IN TEARS BY RICHARD SMALLWOOD)

There are several principles about sowing and reaping, according to the word of God:

Be not deceived; God is not mocked: for whatsoever a man soweth, that shall he also reap. For he that soweth to his flesh shall of the flesh reap corruption; but he that soweth to the Spirit shall of the Spirit reap life everlasting. (Galatians 6:7-8 - KJV).

Remember this: whoever sows sparingly will also reap sparingly, and whoever sows generously will also reap generously. (2 Corinthians 9:6 - NIV).

Those who sow with tears will reap with songs of joy. Those who go out weeping, carrying seed to sow, will return with songs of joy, carrying sheaves with them. (Psalm 126:5-6 - NIV).

It can be considered the law of nature, that whatever seed you put in the ground, that is the fruit you will reap. Wherever you plant it, that is where it shall spring up. However, when it comes to sowing into the lives of people, where you sow it, you may not reap it. In other words, you shall reap what you sow, but it may not come from the same ground. Stop disappointing yourself expecting the same people you bless, to bless you back. Sometimes when you consider the persons you invested in, the places you laboured, the long hours you put in, the contributions you made, the lives you impacted, the friends you were always there for, the help you offered, the sacrifices you made and there is nothing in return but ungratefulness and disrespect, you may not be encouraged to continue.

> *Let us not become weary in doing good, for at the proper time we will reap a harvest if we do not give up. (Galatians 6:9 - NIV).*

You cannot expect people to operate like the "seedtime and harvest" principle; they will change and so will their attitudes. Not everyone you invest in will invest back in you. God will cause you to sow in one ground and reap from another. The moment you stop expecting the returns, but just do as the Lord leads, then you will start to look to Him for your reward.

> *A generous person will prosper; whoever refreshes others will be refreshed. (Proverbs 11:25 - NIV).*

It is about "what you sow" and not "where you sow." Those same seeds will come back up to you in the form of blessings. The Scripture says: "what a man sows..." and not: "where a man sows." Stop confusing yourself with the "where" that is not springing up anything for you to benefit from. What you sow in the lives of people will come back to you, even through others who you did nothing for.

If you are truly giving and helping from your heart, you don't stand around with hands folded waiting for the same people to be of help to you as well. As unfair as it seems, no one is obligated to you because you helped them. Start looking to reap what you have sown elsewhere. Do not miss your breakthrough by looking to the wrong people for help. Funny enough, the persons you should help are the ones who will not give anything back.

> *If you love those who love you, what credit is that to you? Even sinners love those who love them. And if you do good to those who are good to you, what credit is that to you? Even sinners do that. And if you lend to those from whom you expect repayment, what credit is that to you? Even sinners lend to sinners, expecting to be repaid in full. But love your enemies, do good to them, and lend to them without expecting to get anything back. Then your reward will be great, and you will be children of the Most High, because he is kind to the*

> *ungrateful and wicked. (Luke 6:32-35 - NIV).*

In these times, people are careful who they help because of the ungratefulness of others. When you shut up your bowels of compassion and your gift of giving, you are sabotaging yourself of what is due to you.

> *In everything I did, I showed you that by this kind of hard work we must help the weak, remembering the words the Lord Jesus himself said: 'It is more blessed to give than to receive.' (Acts 20:35 - NIV).*

It may not come from where you have sown it, but it will come from somewhere back to you. If your own refuses you, the Lord gives you His love. Just keep sowing good seeds. What you sow into the lives of others, will be sown back into your life by that divinely assigned person. **You will reap from places you have never sown.**

> *Give, and it will be given to you. A good measure, pressed down, shaken together and running over, will be poured into your lap. For with the measure you use, it will be measured to you. (Luke 6:38 - NIV).*

Again, it is what you sow that will come back to you with the same measure. If you sow love, peace, kindness, patience and mercy, you will reap those things in your life. If you sow strife, jealousy, bitterness and condemnation, you will reap those back.

People may never say "thank you" or "well done." Do not allow emotions to get in the way of your sowing. Sometimes, it is because of their ungratefulness why you got double elsewhere. Whatever you do secretly, God will reward you openly. (See Matthew 6:4). You can never surpass God's giving. When you give, you give to the Lord. You may not reap where you sow, but what you sow, you will reap.

Day 42
You Can Grow Among Thorns

(Song to listen: In The Valley by The Martin's Heritage)

No one likes to be pricked, more so, to be surrounded by thistles and thorns. This great discomfort can ruin any good thing by stifling its growth. Growing in conditions where you feel trapped, burdened, and in constant pain, produced by nagging thorns, can never be a good experience. Your mind may be more on the discomfort, than it is on the growth. Could it really be in the will of God for you to grow among thorns? What lesson or experience would God really want you to get from being surrounded by thorns?

Paul had one in his side and that was a nightmare for him, so he begged the Lord to take it out.

> *Three times I pleaded with the Lord to take it away from me. But he said to me, "My grace is sufficient for you, for my power is made perfect in weakness." Therefore I will boast all the more gladly about my weaknesses, so that Christ's power may rest on me. (2 Corinthians 12:8-9 - NIV).*

The Lord will keep you in a thorny situation, just to prove that you can grow with it, through it or pass it. For some of us, we will have to outgrow our thorns to come out. No one likes discomfort, but you may have to press and endure it for your growth. The Lord did not place you among the thorns to suffocate and die, but to thrive and grow. They cause discomfort, but don't allow them to affect your growth.

Many are still fascinated as to how a beautiful thing as a rose, grows among thorns. It remains in its splendour and beauty throughout its growth process. You can stand out among the thorns. You can grow beautifully in the grace of God, even among things that could ruin you.

> *Do everything without grumbling or arguing, so that you may become blameless and pure, "children of God without fault in a warped and crooked generation." Then you will shine among them like stars in the sky. (Philippians 2:14-15 - NIV)*

You don't have to look like what you are going through; God beautifies the meek with salvation. (See Psalm 149:4). You can grow as poised and radiant as ever among those thorns in your life that have fenced you in. The thorns are also God's way of guarding you from outside attacks. Satan realized there was a hedge around Job:

> *Hast not thou made an hedge about him, and about his house, and about all that he*

hath on every side? Thou hast blessed the work of his hands, and his substance is increased in the land. (Job 1:10 - KJV).

The thorns will soon turn into your defence. The more the thorns surround you, the less exposed you are to the plan of the enemy. Therefore, the thorn is really a protection for the rose. What have the thorns become in your life; a blessing or a burden—protection or provocation?

Stray animals struggle to reach through the thorns to get to the rose. They won't get to you easily through the thorns. **The thorns are your experiences building your testimonies**. When Paul got the revelation, he declared:

> *Therefore I will boast all the more gladly about my weaknesses, so that Christ's power may rest on me. (2 Corinthians 12:9b - NIV).*

If the thorns around cannot destroy you, and the thorns on the inside cannot stop you, then nothing on the outside will devour you. Let nothing stop you from growing; outgrow your thorns.

Day 43
When God Gets Silent

(Song to listen: We Need To Hear From You by Andre Crouch)

When God gets silent, there is chaos. When no words seem to be coming through, the worrying begins. Yet, even in His silence, He is still speaking, working and moving. But His silence is your problem.

The moment He is not saying anything on the matter you want Him to address, you believe He is not answering your prayers. Impatience often lead you to another source for answers. Why does the believer get so uneasy in God's silence?

When God gets silent, He starts speaking through other things; if you don't hear His voice, you will see his hand. He always speaks through the pages of the Bible. Situations, encounters and even a song, carry the voice of God. Trust His silence and seek Him continually, because He could be speaking.

If and when He goes silent, there is no need to panic. Many times, you start to look for failures within yourself that could be causing God's silence. You examine your life and the things you have said or done recently. So, you go into fasting and prayer; consecrating yourself, and when you still hear nothing from God, you begin to doubt Him. Sometimes His silence has nothing to do with you falling short of His Glory. He may be testing your patience, stillness and your ability to trust Him when you can't hear Him.

In an exam room, the invigilator only speaks to you when necessary. God won't always tell you what to do, as you were already taught, trained and instructed. So, He may go silent and observe you. God is confident in your ability to recall and apply what His word says. Victory and success are already yours. The test is set in such a way where: *"...he will not let you be tempted beyond what you can bear. But when you are tempted, he will also provide a way out so that you can endure it."* (1 Corinthians 10:13b - NIV).

Silence is powerful and can be interpreted in many ways. It is also a weapon of defence. **I remember I was experiencing a fight, and I sought the Lord and I got no instructions from Him. He got silent on me, so I would be silent in the battle. In my strategy of silence, I overcame the enemy.** God will go silent sometimes for you to go silent; be still and stop talking. Knowing when to speak and when not to speak is an art of a great warrior.

The Lord told Joshua to march around the walls of the city of Jericho seven times without a shout:

> *Do not give a war cry, do not raise your voices, do not say a word until the day I tell you to shout. Then shout! (Joshua 6:10b - NIV).*

God is teaching you something about silence. Silence is powerful; it is obedience and it is a defence. When there is no sound, observe the signs because work is still in progress.

While God is silent, be careful who or what you take instructions from. It is in this silence that everything else begins to speak to you in order to confuse you. Be careful not to take matters in your own hands as well. Be keen and observant, listening to the spirit of the Lord. Do not take His silence for consent. If God is not saying anything about it, it doesn't mean He is in agreement or giving you approval. He could be silent for you to find His voice in His word. He may not send someone to warn or prophecy to you like Nathan with David, but His instruction remains the same as what you already know in His word.

Ensure that when God gets ready to speak to you, it is not in instant judgment or the last time He will have to speak to you on the matter. He may not even be silent as you believe, but you are not listening to hear him. Don't just listen for His voice; observe His hand. God is still speaking.

Day 44
Stretchable But Not Breakable

(Song to listen: Look At Me by Kerrian Johnson)

You are being stretched but will not break. You are feeling the pressure of the pulling, but you will not lose shape. You are taking back your form. Just like an elastic band, you are returning to your original shape and form.

It is not going to wear you out and cause you to lose your spiritual elasticity. You are bouncing back from the set back. You are regaining your strength and restoring your feathers to fly again.

Eagles are full of life and are visionaries, but they find time to look back at their life and re-energize themselves. This happens at about the age of thirty. What happens is that when the eagles reach the age of thirty, their physical body condition deteriorates fast, making it difficult for them to survive. What is really interesting is that the eagle never gives up living, instead it retreats to a mountaintop and over a five-month period goes through a metamorphosis. It knocks off its own beak by banging it against a rock, plucks out its talons and then feathers. Each stage produces a re-growth of the removed body parts, allowing the eagle to live for another 30 - 40 years.[4]

Like an eagle, you are created to last. The Lord has come that you may have life and life more abundantly (See John 10:10).

The Lord, *"satisfies your desires with good things so that your youth is renewed like the eagle's." (Psalm 103:5 - NIV).*

You will not breakdown because, *"those who hope in the Lord will renew their strength. They will soar on wings like eagles; they will run and not grow weary, they will walk and not be faint." (Isaiah 40:31 - NIV).*

You have the ability, through the grace of God, to build up a resistance to anything that comes to pull on your strength and stretch your firmness out of place. A resistance to anything that presses, twists, moves you beyond the limit and over the boundary. The Lord will extend your vitality, endurance, strength and flexible with every stretch. God may allow the stretching because He knows you will not break apart. Jesus told Peter that the devil desires to sift him as wheat, but when he returns to his form, he should strengthen his brothers.

> *Simon, Simon, Satan has asked to sift all of you as wheat. But I have prayed for you, Simon, that your faith may not fail. And*

---

[4] nairaland.com

> when you have turned back, strengthen your brothers. (Luke 22:31-32 - NIV).

You will take back your form, because God will be with you to ensure you don't break apart, even if He allows them to stretch you. You may feel as if you are at your breaking point, but you are going to be surprised to see how far you could be stretched without breaking. God decides your breaking point, not you. You shall stand the test of time.

> No temptation has overtaken you except what is common to mankind. And God is faithful; he will not let you be tempted beyond what you can bear. But when you are tempted, he will also provide a way out so that you can endure it. (1 Corinthians 10:13 - NIV).

The clay by itself can break apart easily under pressure, but the Spirit of the Lord in you makes you stretchable and not breakable. Like Jabez, if you are telling God to enlarge your territories or borders, get ready to be stretched. If you are put in the fire to burn, it is just to reform you; you will not be consumed. Every time you see yourself pulling through, coming out, getting back up, bouncing back, instead of breaking down or apart, it is the elasticity of the grace of God in you. It has the ability to keep pulling you back.

The Spirit of God keeps you stretching without breaking, the word keeps you enduring, and His grace keeps pulling you back. They thought they could break you, but you are too stretchable; you keep forming back. The persecutions could not tear you apart, because someone stronger is within you.

> *But we have this treasure in jars of clay to show that this all-surpassing power is from God and not from us. We are hard pressed on every side, but not crushed; perplexed, but not in despair; persecuted, but not abandoned; struck down, but not destroyed. (2 Corinthians 4:7-9 - NIV).*

You were built to last.

Day 45
Show Him Where You Buried It

(SONG TO LISTEN: FOUR DAYS LATE BY ELEANOR RILEY)

Jesus showed up four days later and told the mourning family to show Him where Lazarus was buried.

> *When Jesus saw her weeping, and the Jews who had come along with her also weeping, he was deeply moved in spirit and troubled. "Where have you laid him?" he asked. "Come and see, Lord," they replied. Jesus wept. (John 11:33-35 - NIV)*

Jesus was intentionally four days late, then showed up declaring He is the resurrection and the life.

> *Jesus said to her, "Your brother will rise again." Martha answered, "I know he will rise again in the resurrection at the last day." Jesus said to her, "I am the resurrection and the life. The one who believes in me will live, even though they die." (John 11:23-25 - NIV).*

Jesus, while at the place where Lazarus was buried, told them to roll the stone away. Martha had to remind Him that He showed up four days late.

> *"Take away the stone," he said. "But, Lord," said Martha, the sister of the dead man, "by this time there is a bad odor, for he has been there four days." (John 11:39 - NIV).*

Similarly, when we have a dying situation and we call on Jesus, we expect Him to show up right away before it gets worse. We try to wait like He said we should, but days turned into years. Therefore, many of us, because of His delay, call it dead and bury it. Jesus did not appear, so all hope is gone. He will intentionally delay to work a miracle for you. He will delay to show you that He is the resurrection and the life and nothing dead will stay dead when He shows up. Be careful not to bury what God still sees life in. I believe one of the reasons Jesus delayed was because, to Him, Lazarus was just sleeping.

> *After he had said this, he went on to tell them, "Our friend Lazarus has fallen asleep; but I am going there to wake him up." His disciples replied, "Lord, if he sleeps, he will get better." Jesus had been speaking of his death, but his disciples thought he meant natural sleep. (John 11: 11-13 - NIV).*

What if the thing is really sleeping and you buried it? The Lord wanted you to still believe in it, but you put it where it can rot and decay.

The Lord is asking: "Where have you buried it?" He is coming to enquire about what He placed in, entrusted in your care, and given you authority over. It is a dishonour to the Lord for Him to come and find it buried.

> *Then the man who had received one bag of gold came. 'Master,' he said, 'I knew that you are a hard man, harvesting where you have not sown and gathering where you have not scattered seed. So I was afraid and went out and hid your gold in the ground. See, here is what belongs to you.' His master replied, 'You wicked, lazy servant! So you knew that I harvest where I have not sown and gather where I have not scattered seed? Well then, you should have put my money on deposit with the bankers, so that when I returned I would have received it back with interest.' (Matthew 25:24-27 - NIV).*

Many have buried the will of God to achieve their desires.

> *What good will it be for someone to gain the whole world, yet forfeit their soul? Or what can anyone give in exchange for their soul? (Matthew 16:26 - NIV).*

What have you buried because God did not appear when you called? He wants an account of it. Show Him where you buried it. Maybe, for you, you have buried yourself because of the condemnation of others. Jesus is at your graveside. The stone must be rolled away. Jesus is removing the stone of bitterness and resentment in your heart caused by the evil acts against you. He is calling you forth. Take off the grave clothes and walk free. He is about to resurrect your hope, joy, peace, confidence, visions, dreams, gifts and give you renewed strength.

Everything buried must be shown to Him. Show Him the places you have hidden them; yes, show Him the secret burial ground and the dead stuff in your life you never talk about. It is resurrection time.

Day 46
Let Down Your Tail

(SONG TO LISTEN: BRING ME DOWN BY GRACE THRILLERS)

You are as proud as a peacock—let down your tail. To be "proud as a peacock" means vain or self-centred—it describes arrogance, vanity or boastfulness.[5]

It is said that when a male peacock sees another peacock it desires, it entices it by spreading its tail feathers as wide as possible in a glorious fan pattern; showing off itself in a prideful way.

King Solomon wrote that he had seen it all and there was no benefit to boast in vanity:

> *Then I looked on all the works that my hands had wrought, and on the labour that I had laboured to do: and, behold, all was vanity and vexation of spirit, and there was no profit under the sun. (Ecclesiastes 2:11 - KJV).*

---

[5] thefreedictionary.com

It is very easy to boast in your own achievements and to feel dignified in your own possessions; but God is not pleased with your pridefulness.

> *Wherefore he saith, God resisteth the proud, but giveth grace unto the humble. (James 4:6b - KJV).*

> *The Lord Almighty planned it, to bring down her pride in all her splendor and to humble all who are renowned on the earth. (Isaiah 23:9 - NIV).*

> *This is what the Lord says: "Let not the wise boast of their wisdom or the strong boast of their strength or the rich boast of their riches." (Jeremiah 9:23 - NIV).*

Let down your tail:

> *Humble yourselves before the Lord, and he will lift you up. (James 4:10 - NIV).*

> *When pride comes, then comes disgrace, but with humility comes wisdom. (Proverbs 11:2 - NIV).*

The humble takes corrections, follows instructions and desires to learn. The humble learn to, *"Do nothing out of selfish ambition or vain conceit. Rather, in humility value others above yourselves." (Philippians 2:3).* In pride, you can resist good counsel. Help keeps coming your way, but pride keeps showing up. God wants to exalt you, but pride is in the way. He wants to reveal some things to you, but not until you are poor in spirit.

> *Blessed are the poor in spirit, for theirs is the kingdom of heaven. (Matthew 5:3 - NIV).*

When you become humble, God will exalt you. If you come down, He will show up. You must be weak to feel His strength. He is the only self-sufficient and all-knowing God. All glory belongs to Him. The Lord will not compete or share His glory with another.

You have achieved much, but you can still be humble. If you must boast, let it be in God. If you don't let your tail down, you will miss one of the biggest breakthroughs of your life because it may come through the one you least expect.

> *We do not dare to classify or compare ourselves with some who commend themselves. When they measure themselves by themselves and compare themselves with themselves, they are not wise. We, however, will not boast beyond proper limits, but will confine our boasting to the sphere of service God himself has assigned to us, a sphere that also includes you. But, "Let the one who boasts boast in the Lord." For it is not the one who commends himself who is approved, but*

> the one whom the Lord commends. (2
> Corinthians 10:12-13 & 17-18 - NIV).

If you don't learn to let down your tail, you will stay in that condition—secretly struggling with your tail up. Your deliverance can be hindered by the height of your tail. God may require you to do the unusual and your tail has got to come down.

Naaman was covered in sores. He showed up at Elisha's doorstep for his healing.

> So Naaman went with his horses and chariots and stopped at the door of Elisha's house. Elisha sent a messenger to say to him, "Go, wash yourself seven times in the Jordan, and your flesh will be restored and you will be cleansed." But Naaman went away angry and said, "I thought that he would surely come out to me and stand and call on the name of the Lord his God, wave his hand over the spot and cure me of my leprosy. Are not Abana and Pharpar, the rivers of Damascus, better than all the waters of Israel? Couldn't I wash in them and be cleansed?" So he turned and went off in a rage. (2 Kings 5:9-12 - NIV).

Naaman was a great man; highly esteemed and dignified. He was commander of an army and a brave solider. His master called him great, because through him the Lord had brought victories. (See 2 Kings 5:1). This man wanted his healing but had his tail in his back. He had a high opinion of what was due to him and how his healing experience should have been like. He had an issue with Elisha's instructions and even the river he chose to send him to dip in. God is not influenced or intimated by your titles or positions:

> *For there is no respect of persons with God. (Romans 2:11 - KJV).*

There are times when we may feel we deserve better than what God chooses to bless us with and even how He may choose to deliver us, because of our works or positions. However, if you humble yourself in the hand of God, then He will lift you up. (See James 4:10).

Humility wants to surrender to the will of God—pride wants to stand in the way. Pride questions, criticizes, condemns, exalts itself against the will of God. You have to be careful how you exalt or compare your own righteousness and look down on others in the process. Consider the parable of the Pharisee and the Tax Collector; the Lord delighted in the prayer of the Tax Collector because of his humility. (See Luke 18: 9-14).

God qualifies the call and He approves whom He calls. Your help and call have come so many times. Stop allowing opportunities and breakthroughs to miss you because of that tail in you back.

Day 47
The In-Time And On-Time Move

(Song to listen: Don't Do It Without Me by Paul Morton)

God is operating with time, in-time and on-time. Which one can you catch on to? Many may not move with the in-time move and others may miss the on-time move. Therefore, you must ensure that you see and tap into the in-time move and stay connected for the on-time move of God.

How do you detect the in-time and on-time move of God?

The in-time move is: God moving, speaking, delivering, working miracles, and pouring out supernaturally in a particular moment. Here, your spiritual senses must be active to see, hear, feel and respond to the in-time move of God. There are many persons who show up after a move of God, asking for a move of God. You should be able to discern the in-time move and tap into it.

The woman who had an issue of blood for twelve years may have heard that Jesus was going to pass by. She put herself in a position to be where He was passing that day. The woman intentionally pressed her way through the crowd to touch a moving Jesus; tapping into an in-time move. She was at the right place, at the right time, with the right amount of faith. Seemingly, everywhere Jesus went, He healed someone, so He was sure to have healed someone that day.

The woman did not want to miss her healing, so she tapped in. The atmosphere is already set, Jesus has showed up and He is moving, but you are doubting and complaining, instead of participating. Anything you ask could be yours in this moment. Your faith can grant you the breakthrough you have been waiting for, because God is blessing, healing, and delivering in this season. When you are in the middle of a move of God, you must sense it and move with Him. There is an open Heaven over you in the moment and anything you declare, ask, or seek God for can be yours. It was so overwhelming that even the touch of Jesus' garment was enough to heal the woman. (See Luke 8:44).

Blind Bartimaeus sensed the in-time move of God. This was a passing moment, and he did not want to miss it. Understand that the in-time move of God doesn't last always. There will be times when nothing is happening, and there seems to be no open heaven over you; while there are days when the move of God is so obvious and rich. The Blind man heard that Jesus was passing, so he cried out: *"...Jesus, thou of David, have mercy on me." (Mark 10:47b - KJV)*. Jesus heard him, called him and asked: "What do you want me to do for you?" (See Mark 10:51). He told the Lord that he wanted his sight and in that same moment, he received his sight (See Mark 10: 49-52).

When you see an on-time move of God, you must learn to move with Him. Jesus had to stop at the touch of the woman with the issue of blood and the call of blind Bartimaeus, because they moved with Him in-time.

How do you detect an on-time move of God?

It is like a right on time move. It happens just the time when you need it and not always the time when you ask for it. It is that perfect timing of God for your healing, deliverance and breakthrough. It can even be in the form of an on-time word that fits your situation.

God moving on-time is in His time, leaving you to exercise patience and faith. You must wait on Him to act and fulfil His promise. Jesus showed up four days after the death of His friend, Lazarus, but He was still on time to resurrect him (See John 11: 38-44). No matter what time it is when He shows up, He is always on time. Even when it seems too far gone or already over, the on-time move of God is all you need.

While the in-time move requires your active participation, the on-time move requires your patience and faith in the word of God. Sometimes, He will show up after you have given up on it, to show you that it is never too late for Him to move.

God doesn't move out of time. An in-time move of God can produce an on-time miracle in your life. Tap in.

Day 48
Don't Surrender In A Fight You've Already Won

(Song to listen: I Almost Let Go by Kurt Carr)

Could fear be causing it? You want to give in, give up, quit and surrender to the enemy. The hope you once saw is no longer there; you are losing your strength to fight on. So, you are surrendering in what seems to be swallowing you up.

It makes no sense to you to stay and fight, but what you fail to see is that below the surface, there is victory. The change is happening beneath the hardness. It may not seem as if the wall is coming down but keep marching. You are fighting from victory.

With the Lord, you walk in victory. You approach each trial as an overcomer. You have won, even before you win. You never lose, even in the face of defeat.

> *I have told you these things, so that in me you may have peace. In this world you will have trouble. But take heart! I have overcome the world. (John 16:33 - NIV).*

It is by choice a believer surrenders; when you just can't believe that you are truly victorious, when the reality shows otherwise. But you are surrendering to the enemy with victory in your hands. The Lord already designed it for you to triumph. Your victory is fixed.

> *Ye are of God, little children, and have overcome them: because greater is he that is in you, than he that is in the world. (1 John 4:4 - KJV).*

> *No weapon that is formed against thee shall prosper; and every tongue that shall rise against thee in judgment thou shalt condemn. This is the heritage of the servants of the Lord, and their righteousness is of me, saith the Lord. (Isaiah 54:17 - KJV).*

> *Behold, I give unto you power to tread on serpents and scorpions, and over all the power of the enemy: and nothing shall by any means hurt you. (Luke 10:19 - KJV).*

Even your healing is fixed— *"...with His stripes we are healed." (See Isaiah 53:5).*

Jehoshaphat sought the Lord, and He told him not to be afraid because the battle belongs to God.

> *Ye shall not need to fight in this battle: set yourselves, stand ye still, and see the salvation of the Lord with you, O Judah and*

> *Jerusalem: fear not, nor be dismayed; to morrow go out against them: for the Lord will be with you. (2 Chronicles 20:17 - KJV).*

Don't surrender yet; you will see the victory soon. You are not out there, in it, up against it or going through it alone.

> *For God hath not given us the spirit of fear; but of power, and of love, and of a sound mind. (2 Timothy 1:7 - KJV).*

Too many fearful victors are out there; already victorious, but too fearful to see it. Do you find yourself writing off plans based on how your situation looks? Many are doubting, but declare they are trusting God.

> *Strengthen ye the weak hands, and confirm the feeble knees. Say to them that are of a fearful heart, Be strong, fear not: behold, your God will come with vengeance, even God with a recompence; he will come and save you. (Isaiah 35:3-4 - KJV).*

You have the victory; sleep in peace. You are walking in victory; don't give in. God is with you. He told Joshua:

> *Be strong and very courageous. Be careful to obey all the law my servant Moses gave you; do not turn from it to the right or to the left, that you may be successful wherever you go. Have I not commanded you? Be strong and courageous. Do not be afraid; do not be discouraged, for the Lord*

your God will be with you wherever you go. (Joshua 1:7 & 9 - NIV).

Do not surrender in a storm you are equipped to ride out. Do not give up in a battle that is not yours. If Jesus is onboard, there should be calm; He speaks to the wind.

Day 49
What Do You Have In Your House?

(Song to listen: I Surrender All by George Banton)

> *The wife of a man from the company of the prophets cried out to Elisha, "Your servant my husband is dead, and you know that he revered the Lord. But now his creditor is coming to take my two boys as his slaves." Elisha replied to her, "How can I help you? Tell me, what do you have in your house?" (2 Kings 4:1-2a - NIV)*

She cried out to the prophet for help, but instead he asked her, "...what do you have in your house?" How can this solve her problem? Something similar happened when Elijah went to a widow's house and asked her to bake him a cake first. She had to explain to him that she had nothing but a handful of flour and a little jar of oil left in her house to eat and die. (See 1 Kings 17:11-12).

Elisha wanted to help her, but he wanted something to work with. He wanted to know if she had something for God to multiply. Where there is a need, there should be a seed. I have heard it said like this, "If it doesn't meet your need, then it is a seed." These prophets were encouraging these women to surrender, by faith, something they have locked away in their time of drought to God for a supernatural increase. Something is in your house that can be used as a seed; that is why the man of God asked. What you have left in your house may be nothing to you, but something to God.

> *"Your servant has nothing there at all," she said, "except a small jar of olive oil." (2 Kings 4:2b - NIV).*

God wants what you call "but" or "except."

> *And she said, As the Lord thy God liveth, I have not a cake, but an handful of meal in a barrel, and a little oil in a cruse. (1 Kings 17:12a - KJV).*

If you have a great need right now, answer the question, "What do you have in your house?" It may be your last, but it can be a seed that can bring you the greatest harvest you have ever seen. **God wants to work a miracle with your "nothing but."** The widow had nothing to give her creditors and her sons would be taken from her. Are you in debt? What is in your hand, house, or locked away that you call nothing? God is about to work on your nothingness. He is not intimidated by your emptiness; He wants to be the one to fill you up.

Elisha gave the widow an assignment:

> *Elisha said, "Go around and ask all your neighbors for empty jars. Don't ask for just*

> *a few. Then go inside and shut the door behind you and your sons. Pour oil into all the jars, and as each is filled, put it to one side." (2 Kings 4:3-4 - NIV).*

Elijah gave the widow an assignment:

> *Elijah said to her, "Don't be afraid. Go home and do as you have said. But first make a small loaf of bread for me from what you have and bring it to me, and then make something for yourself and your son." (1 Kings 17:13 - NIV).*

If you are obedient, in this drought, you will reap from your nothing. You must follow the instructions you receive by faith and use what is in your house or possession. You will need to get extra vessels for the increase that is coming to your life. The widow went and borrowed vessels from her neighbors and filled all of them out of the one jar of oil she had. God is ready to do the supernatural, when you are ready to give Him all you have left.

No matter how low we run, there is always something left in the house to prepare. God wants it. Elijah transformed the widow into a businesswoman; she sold her oil and paid off her debts and she and her son lived off the rest. The harvest that is coming back to your house will clear your debts and be enough to live off.

What is inside your house may be the seed for your harvest.

Day 50
If You Don't Talk To God, Then Who?

(SONG TO LISTEN: I MUST TELL JESUS BY SANCHEZ)

When you don't talk to God, who do you talk to? If He is not your burden-bearer, then who is? Who or what do you spend your time with daily? Where do you cast your cares? Who do you ask, seek and what door do you knock? Whose voice do you follow? Who instructs you?

> *My sheep hear my voice, and I know them, and they follow me. (John 10:27 - KJV).*

Does He know your voice, and do you know His?

> *For you are a slave to whatever controls you. (2 Peter 2:19b - NLT).*

When trouble comes, who is your refuge? If you don't talk to God, you are talking to someone or something else. What has happened to the communication and relationship you once had with Him?

> *Then Jesus told his disciples a parable to show them that they should always pray and not give up. (Luke 18:1 - NIV).*

Your prayer life has been affected tremendously. You ask for prayer more than how you pray for yourself. The Father longs to hear from you. Who are you busy talking to? The devil will build conversations with you.

Communicating with the Lord is an impactful aspect of your life. You can avoid temptations through prayer:

> *And lead us not into temptation, but deliver us from evil. (Matthew 6:13a - KJV).*
>
> *Watch ye and pray, lest ye enter into temptation. The spirit truly is ready, but the flesh is weak. (Mark 14:38 - KJV).*

Prayer bars temptations. If you are constantly giving in, check whose instructions you follow. Praying helps you control your tongue. Praying keeps you purified. **If you don't keep talking to the Lord, the devil will keep talking to you.** Prayer connects you to the Spirit.

> *Praying always with all prayer and supplication in the Spirit, and watching thereunto with all perseverance and supplication for all saints. (Ephesians 6:18 - KJV).*

If you talk to family members, friends, counsellors or your leaders before talking to God, then your source is really not Him. How important is prayer to you? Do you listen to hear what He has to say? God wants to hear from you as much as you want to hear from Him.

Morning Meditation is that WORD that keeps your heart hoping and mind believing. It positions you, while creating an atmosphere for the impending shift or move of God.

The Lord God hath given me the tongue of the learned, that I should know how to speak a word in season to him that is weary: he wakeneth morning by morning, he wakeneth mine ear to hear as the learned.

(Isaiah 50:4 - *KJV*)

Who is Ava-Gay Blair?

- Radio Announcer
- Promoter
- Voice-over Talent
- Emcee Extraordinaire
- Motivational Speaker
- Author

Interestingly, I grew up knowing there was a special call of God over my life, because the things I do now are not far from what I was interested in then. At a very young age, when I started my walk with the Lord, my siblings and others from my church would, from time to time, ask me to explain Scriptures in the Bible that they were not clear on. I would look at the Scripture and God would open up my understanding and I would express to them what I did not know before. I knew His hand was on me and that greater was ahead.

Today, I am still amazed at how the Lord chooses to use me. Each message He lays on my heart challenges me before or after I deliver it.

I have never written a book before, but here goes my first one. At the age of thirty, this is a great accomplishment for me. I am blessed and empowered by the meditations in this book and I know you will be too.

Someday, I wish to travel to different countries to speak on various platforms. I know my gift will open doors for me along the way.

> *But as it is written, Eye hath not seen, nor ear heard, neither have entered into the heart of man, the things which God hath prepared for them that love him. (1 Corinthians 2:9 - KJV).*

My desire is to remain humble in the hand of the Lord continually. I believe in encouraging people to be the best version of themselves and who God created them to be. I want to see people align themselves with their destinies and walk in their God-given purpose. That way, they will experience a more fulfilling and meaningful life.

www.ingramcontent.com/pod-product-compliance
Lightning Source LLC
Chambersburg PA
CBHW071445150426
43191CB00008B/1248